Toronto Ontario in Colour Photos, Saving Our History One Photo at a Time

Photography
by Barbara Raué
2012

Series Name:
Cruising Ontario

Book 187: Toronto in Colour

Cover photo: Queen's Park, the site of the Ontario Legislative Building

Series Name: Cruising Ontario
Saving Our History One Photo at a Time
in colour photos

Books Available in Alphabetical Order:
Aberfoyle, Acton, Alton, Amherstburg, Ancaster, Arthur, Aylmer, Ayr, Bloomingdale, Brantford, Burlington, Caledon, Caledonia, Cambridge, Clifford, Conestogo, Delhi, Dorchester to Aylmer, Drayton, Drumbo, Dundas, Eden Mills, Elmira, Elora, Essex, Fergus, Guelph, Hagersville, Hamilton, Hanover, Harriston, Hespeler, Jarvis, Kingston, Kingsville, Kitchener, Linwood, Listowel, London, Lucknow, Mono, Mount Forest, Neustadt, New Hamburg, Niagara-on-the-Lake, Oakville, Orangeville, Orillia, Owen Sound, Palmerston, Peterborough, Petrolia, Port Elgin, Preston, Rockwood, Sarnia, Seaforth, Sheffield, Shelburne, Simcoe, Southampton, St. Jacobs, St. Marys, St. Thomas, Stoney Creek, Stratford, Thamesford, Tillsonburg, Waterdown, Waterford, Waterloo, Welland, Wellesley, Windsor, Wingham, Woodstock

Book 157: Brockville
Book 158: Merrickville
Book 159: Smiths Falls
Book 160: Portland, Newboro
Book 161: Westport & Area
Book 162: Perth
Book 163-166: Belleville
Book 167-168: Port Colborne
Book 169: Erin in Colour
Book 170: Goderich in Colour
Book 171: Sault Ste. Marie
Book 172: Lake Superior
Book 173-176: Thunder Bay
Book 177-179: Paris

Book 180: St. George
Book 182-183: Burford
Book 184: Mt Pleasant, Onondaga, Newport
Book 185-186: Grimsby
Book 187: Toronto in Colour

Other Books by Barbara Raue

Coins of Gold

Arrows, Indians and Love

The Life and Times of Barbara
Volume 1: Inventions That Have Enhanced My Life
Volume 2: Entertainment That I Have Enjoyed
Volume 3: East Coast Trips
Volume 4: Olympics Have Always Intrigued Me
Volume 5: Wonders of the World
Volume 6: Caribbean Cruises We Have Enjoyed
Volume 7: Animals
Volume 8: Storms and Other Major Disasters in My Lifetime
Volume 9: Wars, Terrorist Attacks and Major Disasters

The Cromwell Family Book

Laura Secord Discovered

Daddy Where Are You?

Montana Series
Book 1: Montana Dream
Book 2: Life on the Montana Frontier
Book 3: Montana to Boston and Back
Book 4: Montana Sons Go to War
Book 5: Montana Sons Return From War

Visit Barbara's website to view all of her books
http://barbararaue.ca

Toronto

Toronto, the largest city in Canada, the provincial capital of Ontario, is located in Southern Ontario on the northwestern shore of Lake Ontario. The name *Toronto* is likely derived from the Iroquois word *tkaronto* which means "place where trees stand in the water," referring to the northern end of what is now Lake Simcoe where the Huron planted tree saplings to corral fish.

During the American Revolutionary War, United Empire Loyalists fled from the United States to live on lands north of Lake Ontario. In 1787, the British Crown purchased more than a quarter million acres of land from the Mississaugas of the New Credit, and established a settlement called the Town of York. Lieutenant Governor John Graves Simcoe designated York as the capital of Upper Canada. Fort York was constructed at the entrance of the town's natural harbour where it was sheltered by a long sand-bar peninsula. The town was captured and ransacked by American soldiers in the Battle of York during the War of 1812, and the parliament buildings were set on fire.

In 1834, York became a city and the name was changed to Toronto with a population of 9,000 which included escaped African American slaves and slaves brought by the Loyalists, and also Mohawk leader Joseph Brant. The city grew rapidly through the remainder of the 19th century. After the great Irish famine, a large number of Irish came to the area.

In the 19th century, an extensive sewage system was built, and streets were illuminated with gas lighting. Long-distance railway lines were constructed, including a route linking with the Upper Great Lakes. The Grand Trunk Railway and the Northern Railway of Canada joined in the building of the first Union Station. The railway brought more immigrants, and commerce and industry increased. The Gooderham and Worts Distillery was the world's largest whiskey factory by the 1860s. The harbor provided access to grain and sugar imports used in processing. Expanding port and rail facilities brought in northern timber for export and imported Pennsylvania coal; industry dominated the waterfront for the next 100 years.

Horse-drawn streetcars were replaced by electric ones in 1891. The great fire of 1904 destroyed a large section of downtown Toronto but the city was soon rebuilt with more stringent fire safety laws and the expansion of the fire department.

In 1954, the City of Toronto and twelve surrounding municipalities joined together into a regional government known as Metropolitan Toronto. The postwar boom resulted in rapid suburban development, and the metropolitan government began to manage services that crossed municipal boundaries, including highways, police services, water and public transit. In that year, disaster struck the city when Hurricane Hazel brought high winds and flash flooding causing the deaths of 81 people in the Toronto area, and leaving about 1,900 families homeless.

Toronto covers an area of 630 square kilometres stretching 21 kilometres (13 miles) from north to south and 43 kilometers (27 miles) east to west. The waterfront shoreline is 46 kilometres (29 miles) long. The Toronto Islands and Port Lands extend out into the lake. The city's borders are formed by Lake Ontario to the south, Etobicoke Creek and Highway 427 to the west, Steeles Avenue to the north and the Rouge River and the Scarborough-Pickering Townline to the east. Today the city has a population of 2.6 million people. As Canada's commercial capital, it is home to the Toronto Stock Exchange and some of the nation's largest banks. Toronto hosted the 2015 Pan American Games.

The city is intersected by three rivers and many tributaries: the Humber River in the west end and the Don River east of downtown, and the Rouge River at the city's eastern limits. The many creeks and rivers created large tracts of densely forested ravines, and provided sites for parks and recreational trails. These deep ravines are useful for draining the city's storm sewer system during heavy rains, but sections near the Don River are prone to sudden, heavy floods.

Toronto buildings vary in design and age with many structures dating back to the mid-19th century, while other prominent buildings were built in the first decade of the 21st century.

Toronto is a city of high-rises, having 1,800 buildings over 30 metres (98 feet), most of them are residential having been built in the 1950s, while the central business district contains commercial office towers. Through the 1960s and 1970s, significant pieces of Toronto's architectural heritage were demolished to make way for redevelopment or for parking. Since the 2000s, Toronto is experiencing a period of architectural revival, with several buildings by world-renowned architects having opened. Daniel Libeskind's Royal Ontario Museum addition, Frank Gehry's remake of the Art Gallery of Ontario, and Will Alsop's distinctive Ontario College of Art & Design expansion are among the city's new showpieces.

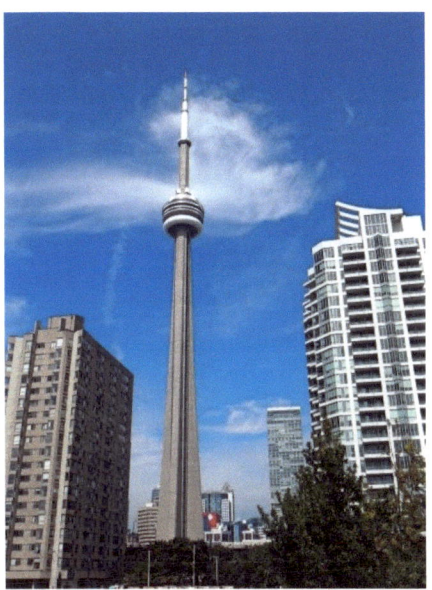

Defining the Toronto skyline is the CN Tower, a telecommunications and tourism hub which was completed in 1976 at a height of 553.33 metres (1,815 feet 5 inches). It was the world's tallest freestanding structure until 2007.

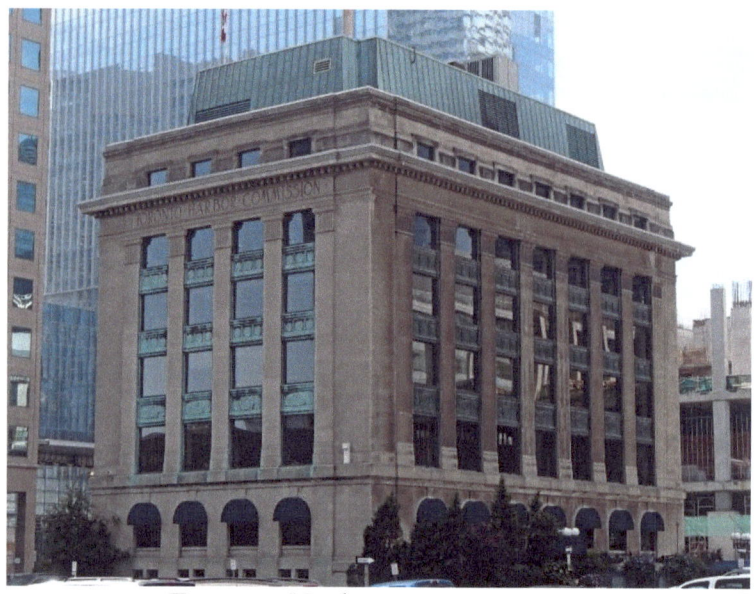
Toronto Harbour Commission

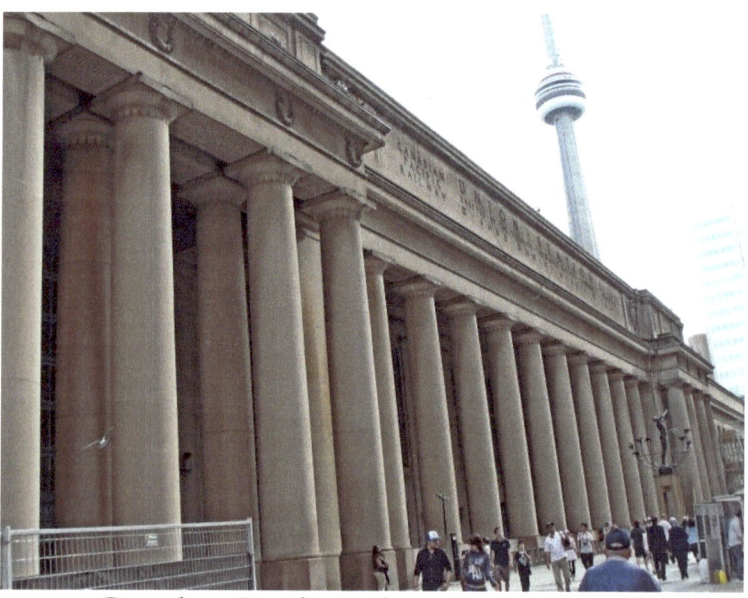
Canadian Pacific Railway Union Station

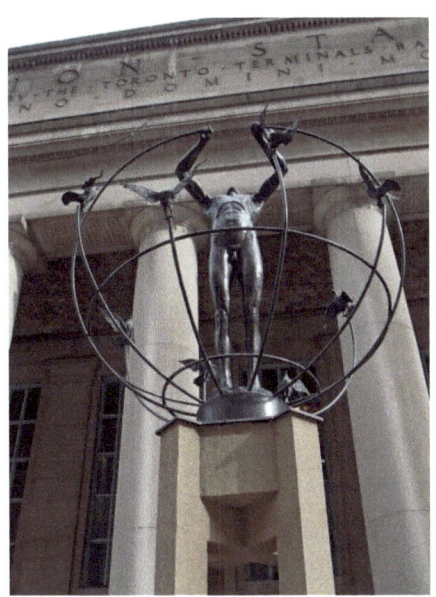

Monument to Multiculturalism unveiled July 1, 1985
Sculpture by Francesco Perilli

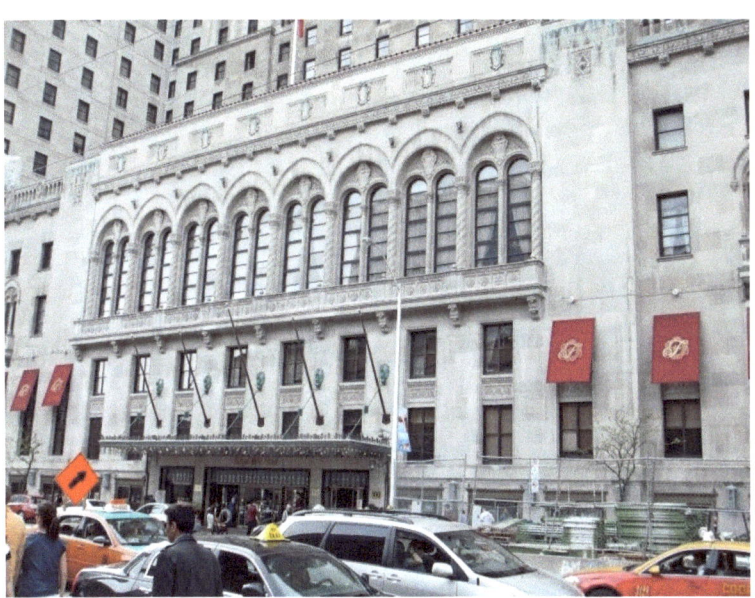

Royal York Hotel

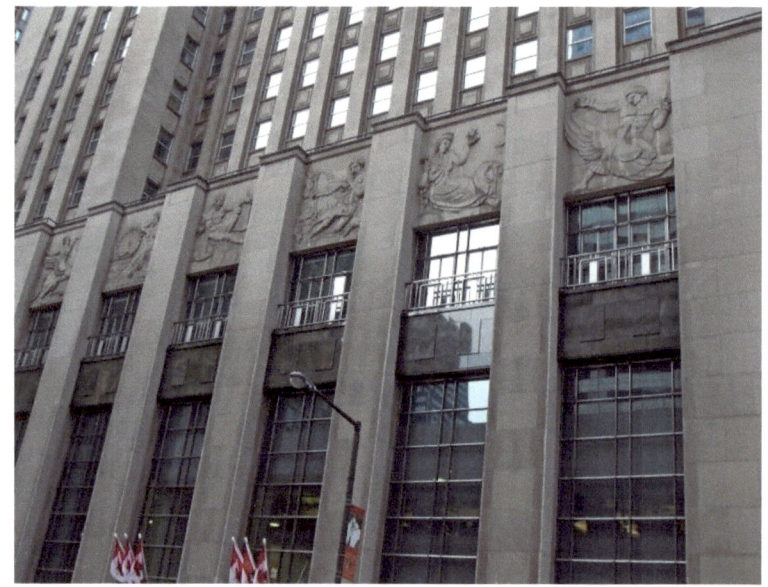

The Bank of Nova Scotia

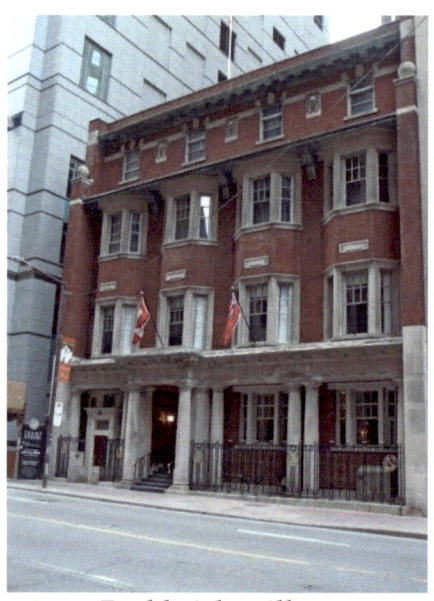

Red brick, pillars

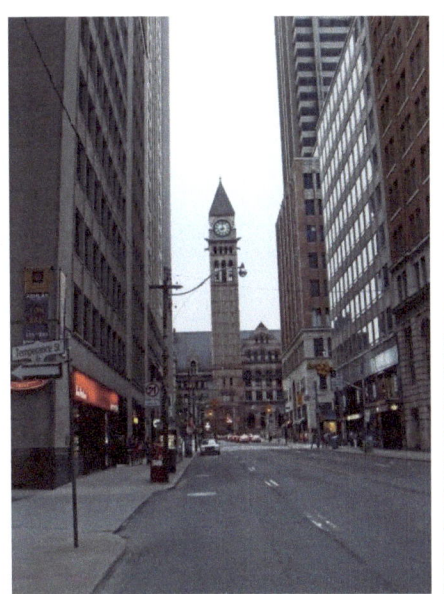
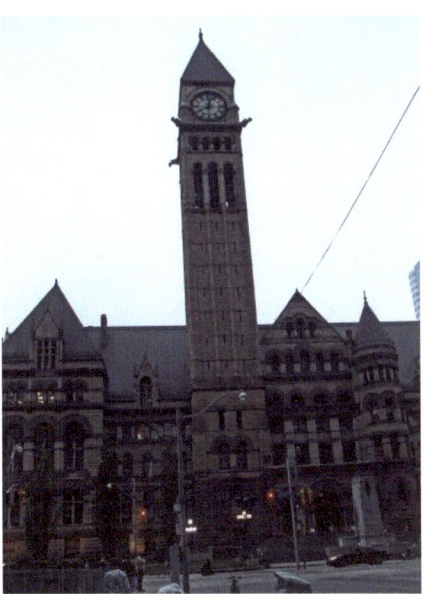

Armouries

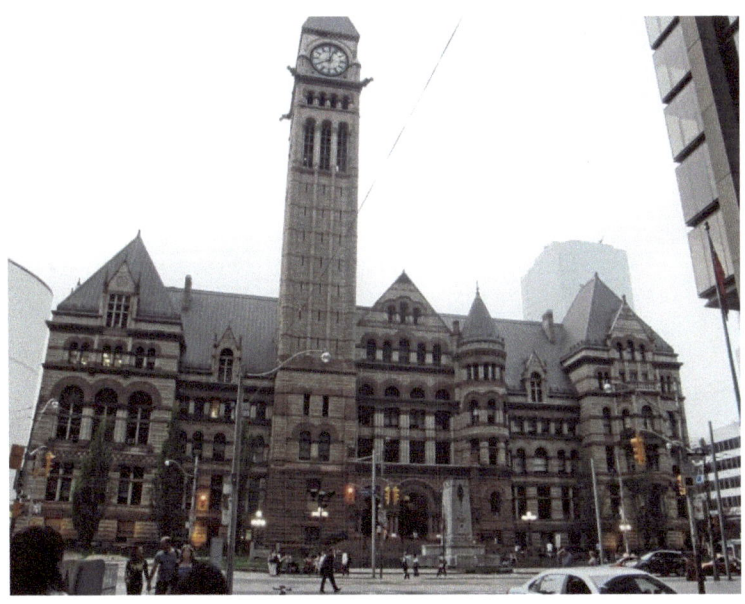

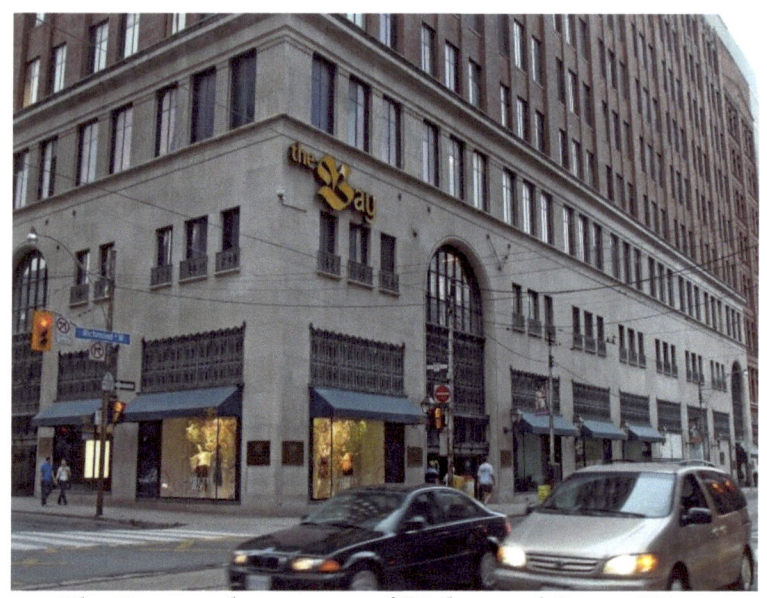

The Bay on the corner of Richmond Street West

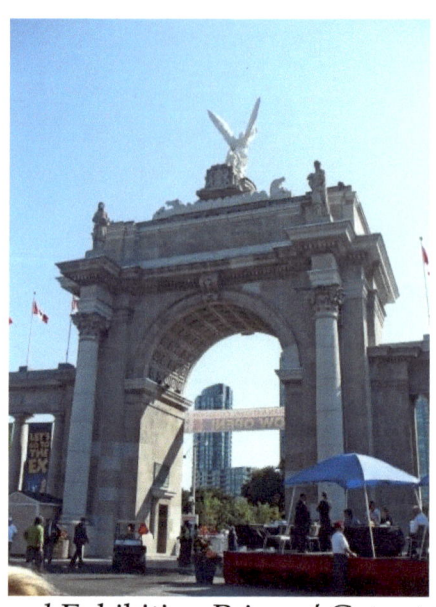

Canadian National Exhibition Princes' Gates triumphal arch – Neo-Classical style - 1927

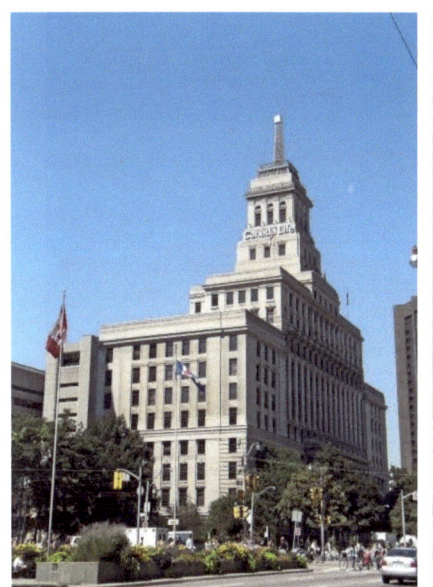 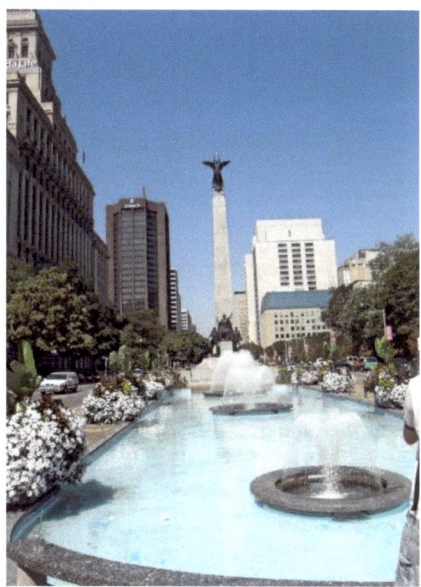

Canada Life building

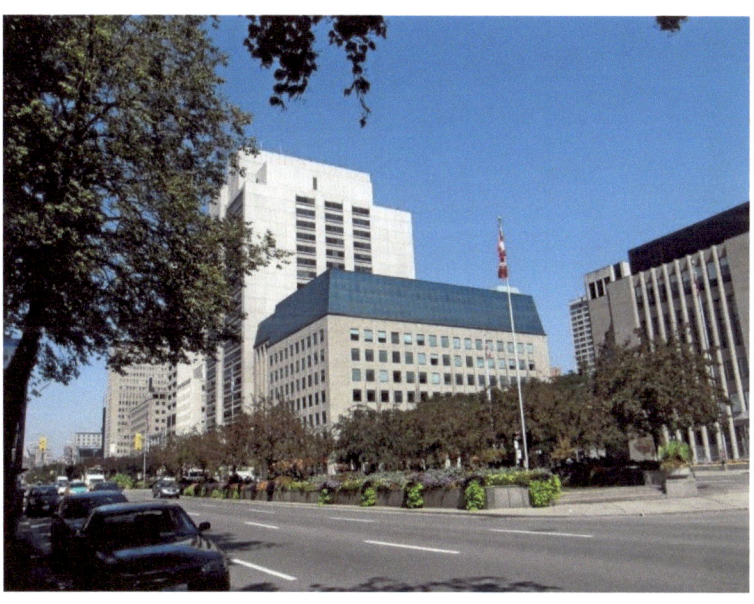

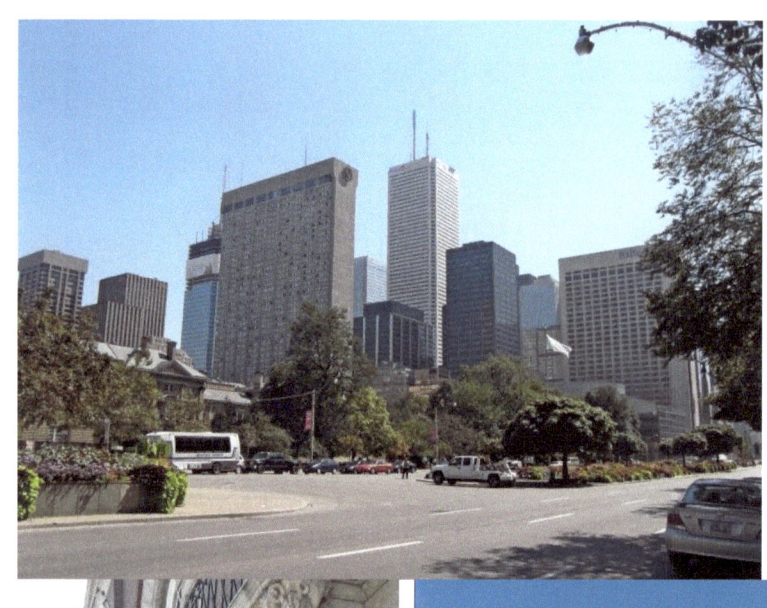

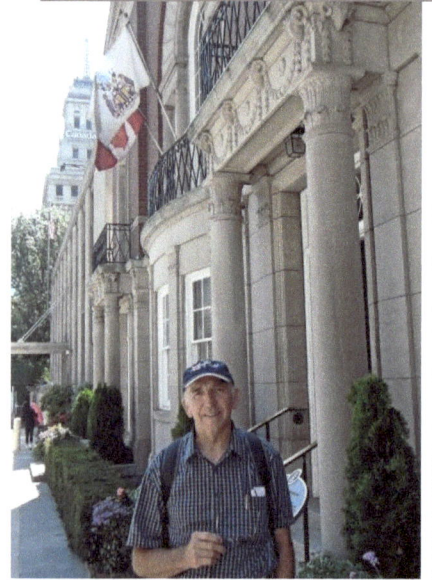
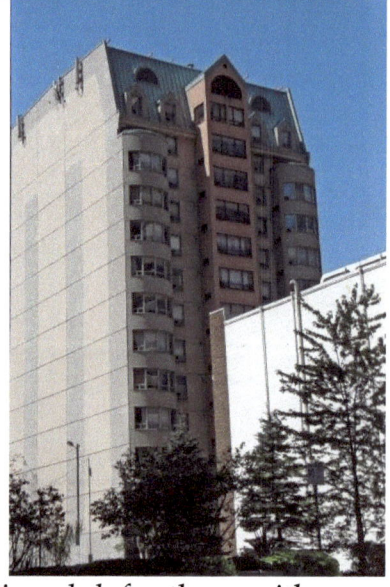

Founded in 1906 as a private dining club for those with a university degree, University Club of Toronto moved to this location on University Avenue in 1929. The club featured dining facilities, a billiard room, library, three squash courts, an oyster bar and nineteen rooms for overnight guests.
    Adamesque Neo-Georgian architecture

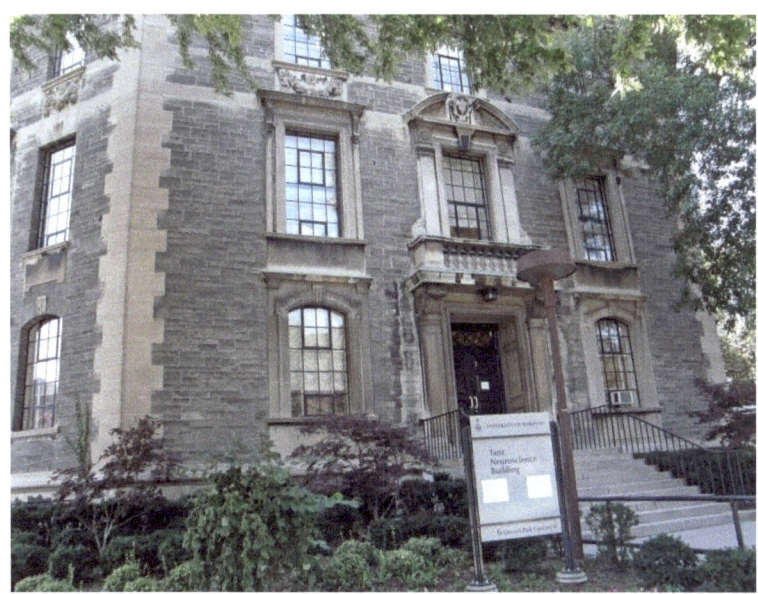

Tanz Neuroscience Building

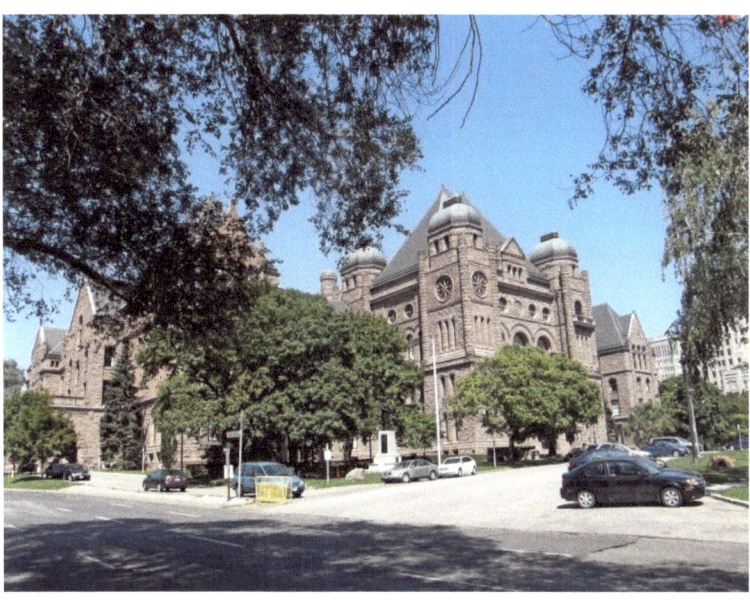

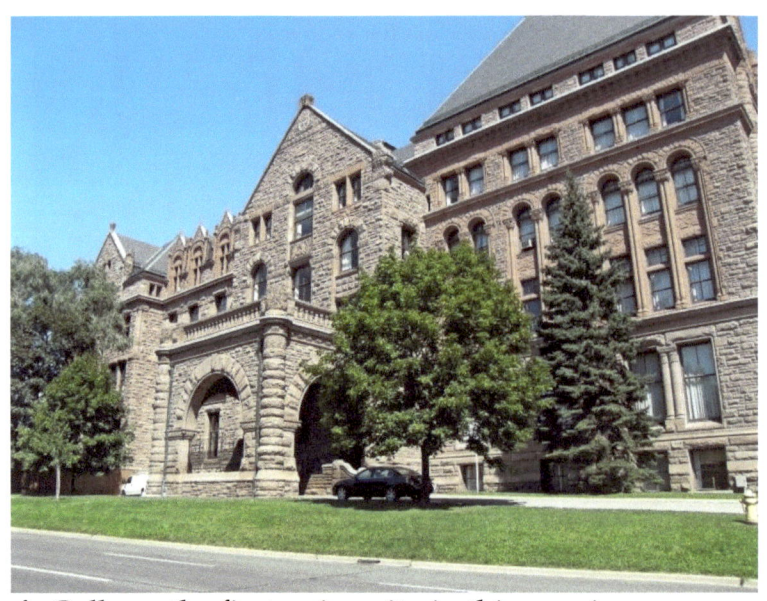

King's College, the first university in this province was chartered in 1827 but it wasn't until 1843 that classes began in the former Parliament Buildings on Front Street. Construction was completed in 1845. King's College offered instruction in the arts, science, law, theology and medicine. In 1850 it became the new University of Toronto.

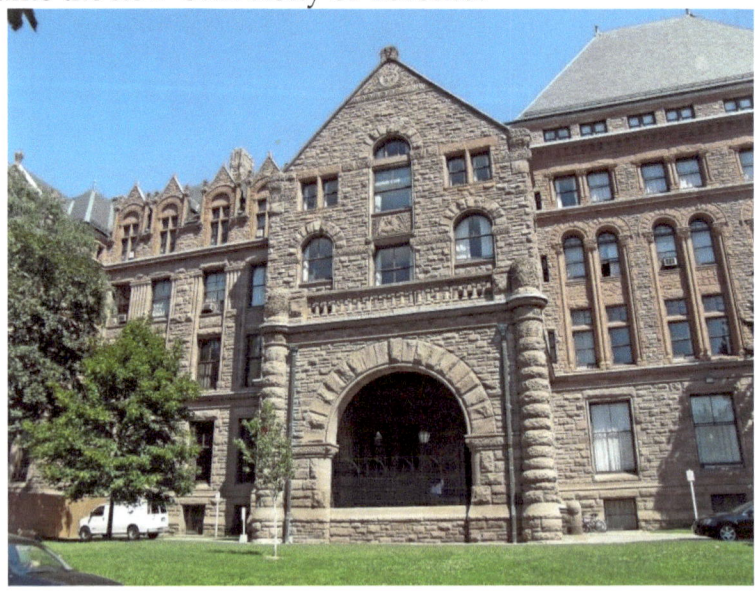

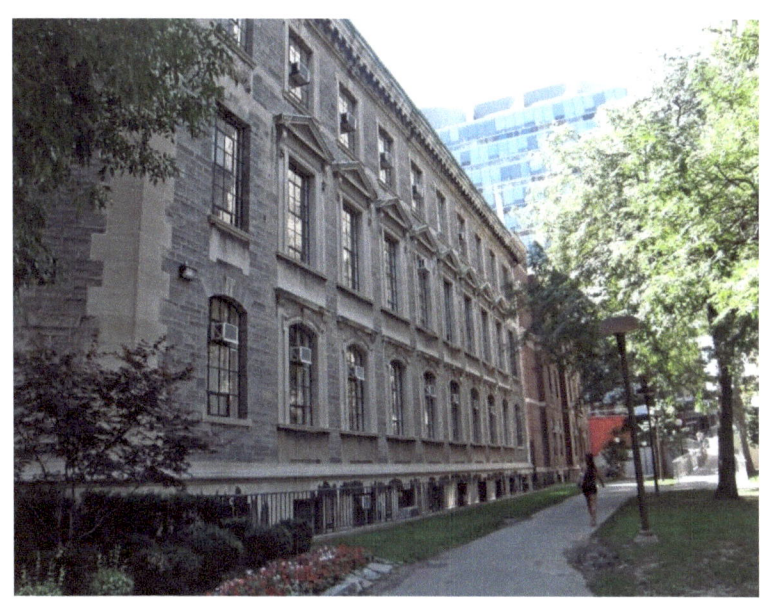

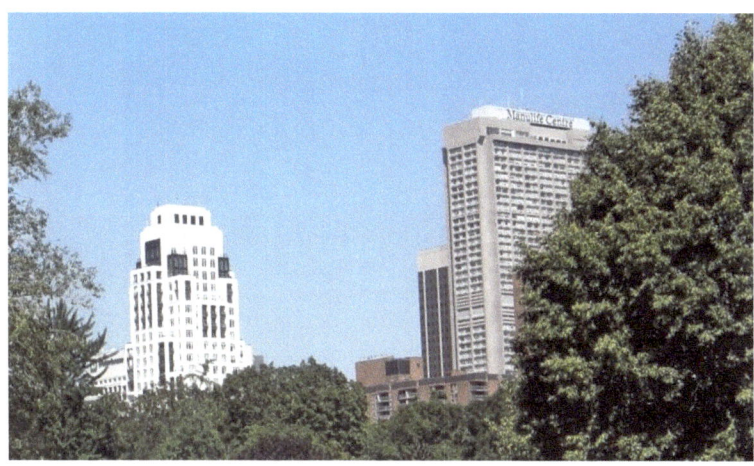

A Trip to the Royal Ontario Museum

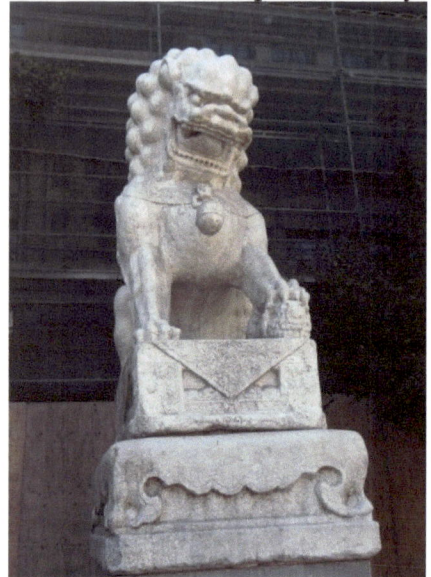
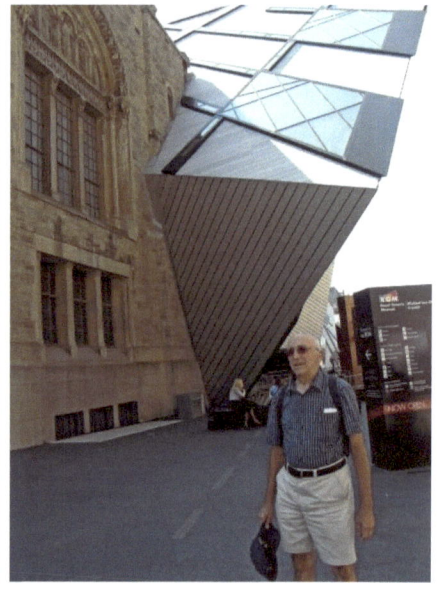

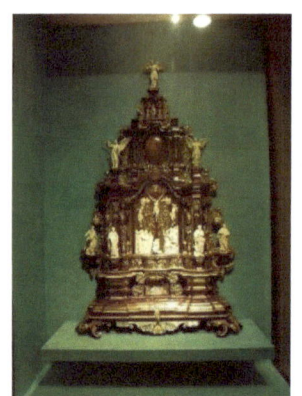
House Alter

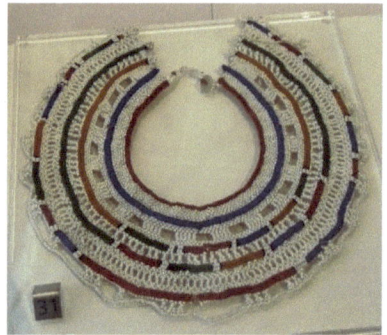
Necklace, South Africa, Beads, thread, 20th Century

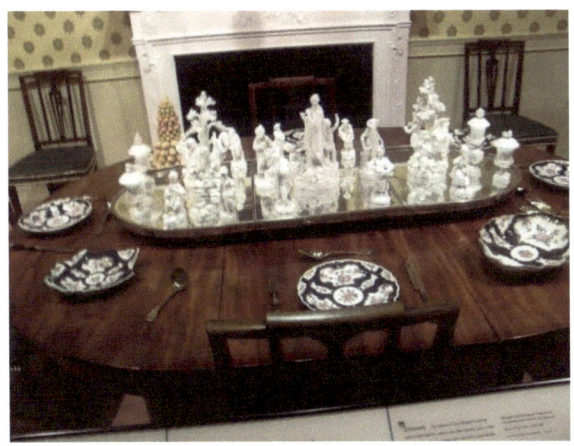

A Regency Tent Room – in the late 1700s the ideals of ancient Greece and Rome were greatly admired. Every aspect of the decorative arts, even the forms of furniture, imitated the ancient world. In France this interpretation of Neo-classicism is known as Empire style. In Britain, it is known as Regency style, in recognition of George, Prince of Wales, later George IV, who was Regent (1813-1820) and an admirer of French fashions. Rooms of the Regency period were more richly appointed than earlier Neo-classical interiors. To simulate ancient interiors, some designers hung rooms with draperies. This condition continued in France and England until the 1830s.

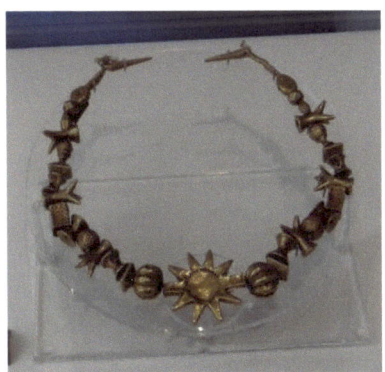

Ghana gold necklace 19th century

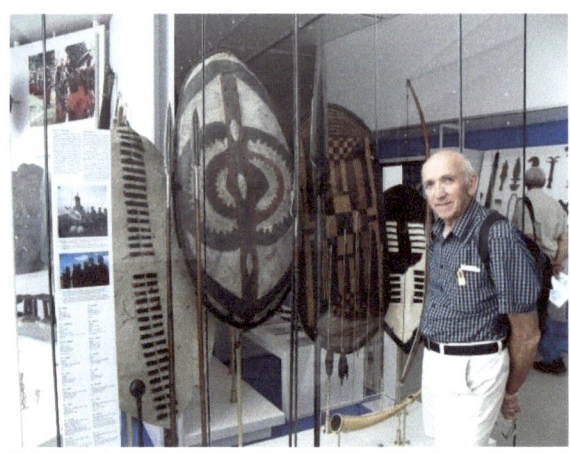

      Shields and weapons were essential instruments of warfare throughout Africa. Even today, among many cultures, the warrior is the quintessential image of African manhood and weapons an essential element of proper manly attire. The possession of swords and daggers is also a visible statement of the political supremacy of leaders and their power of life and death over their subjects. However, even among the most hierarchical and autocratic pre-colonial African states kingship was not the result of mere military superiority, but was grounded in powerful mystical forces that made victories and conquests possible.

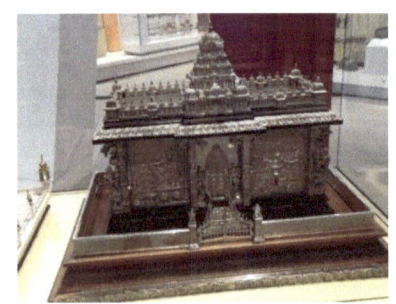 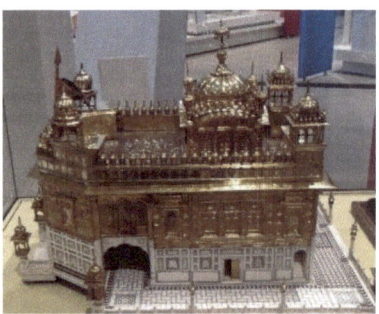

Model of South Indian Temple   Model of Golden Temple

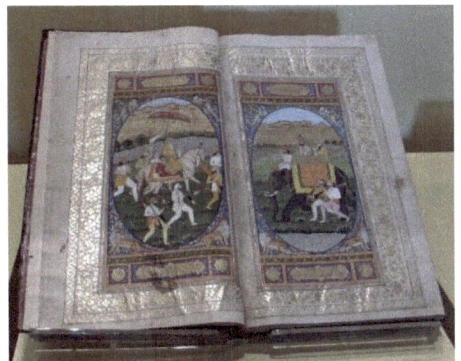
The Chronicles of Emperor Akbar

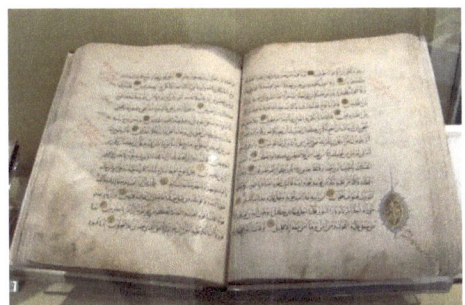
The Qu'ran

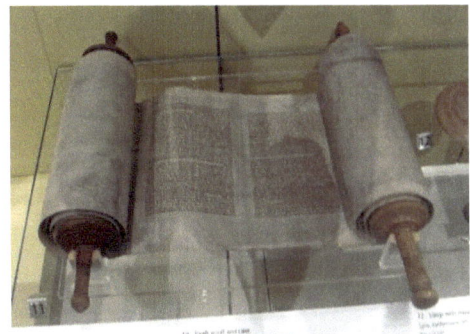
Torah Scroll

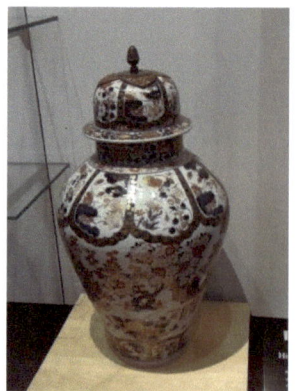

Hizen Ware - designs in blue applied before firing and glazing, decorations with colored enamels and gold applied after firing and glazing

There was a very impressive display of dinosaurs.

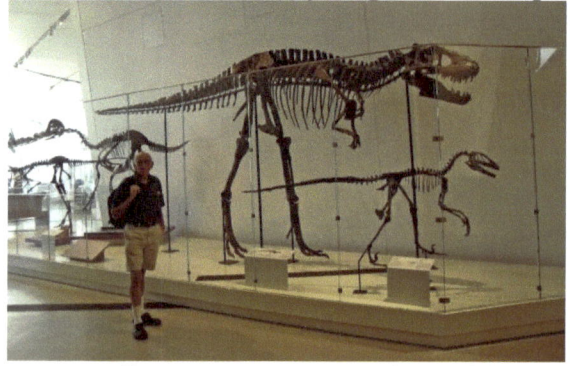 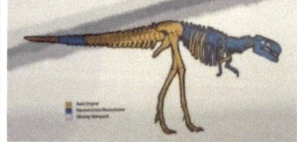

Albertosaurus was adapted for running down prey and using brute force to subdue it. It had a large head and sharp, serrated teeth that must have been capable of ripping through the muscles and bones of the largest prey. The structure of its jaw allowed all the teeth to engage at once when biting. It probably had good vision and a keen sense of smell. The function of its tiny front limbs is unknown.

Yellow = real   Blue = reconstructed

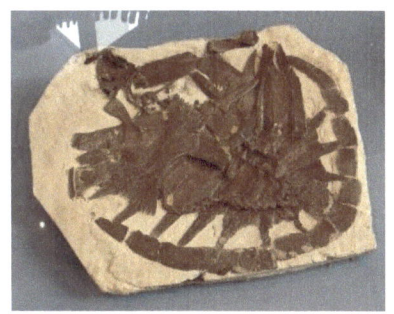
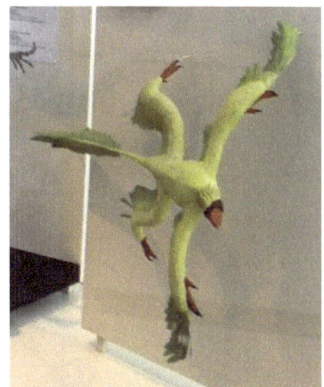

Fossil

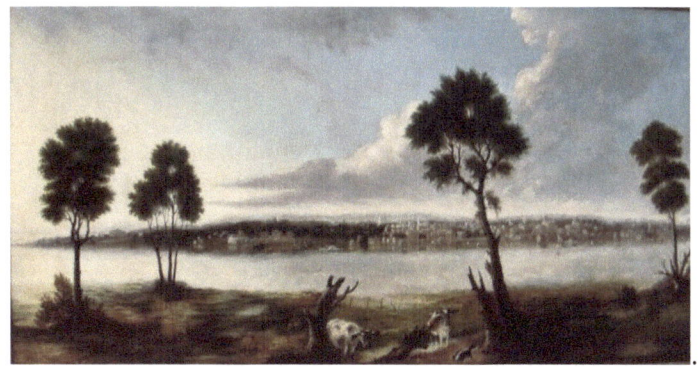

View of Toronto c. 1850

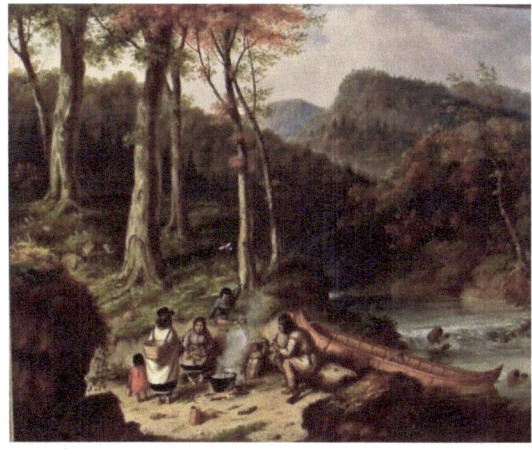

Huron Indians at a Portage by Cornelius Krieghoff

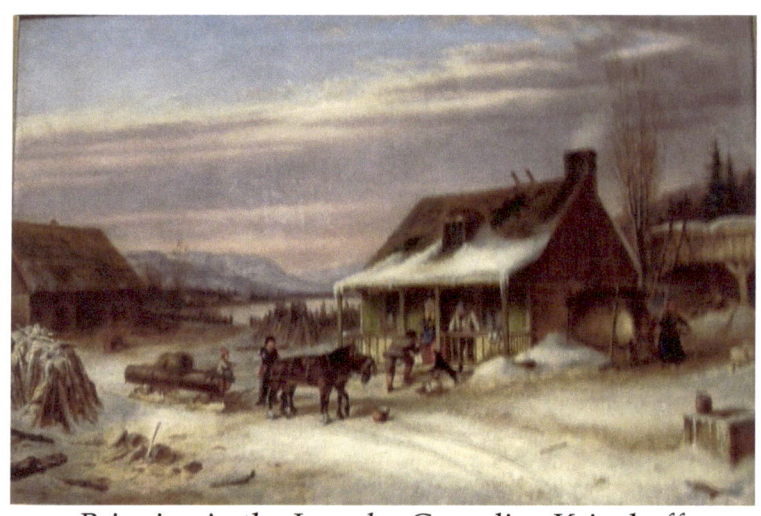
Bringing in the Logs by Cornelius Krieghoff

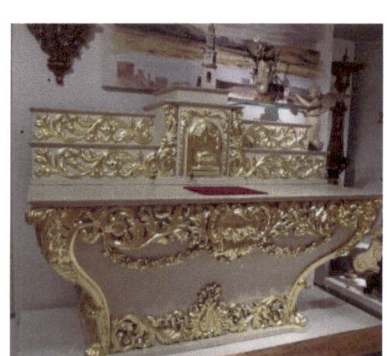
Altar as furniture

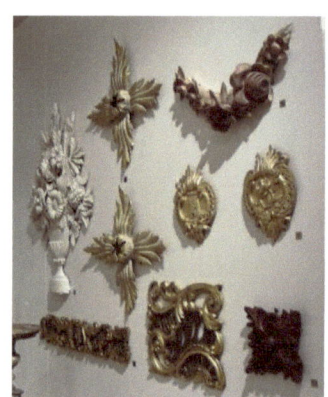
Ornamental wood carvings

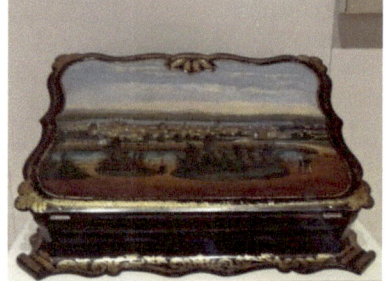
Ladies' writing box with view of Montreal

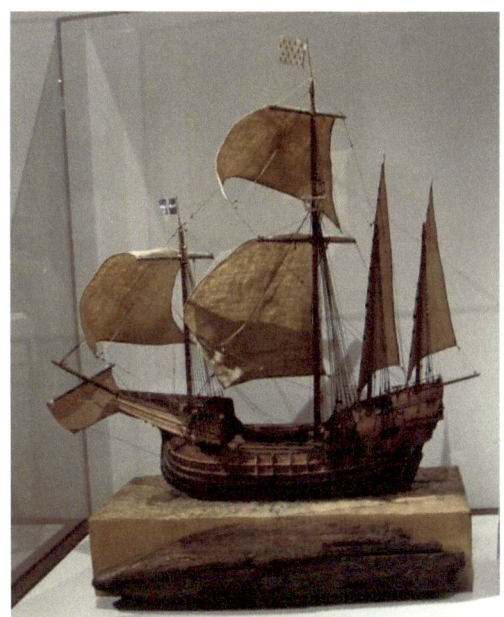

La Grande Hermine, one of Jacques Cartier's ships

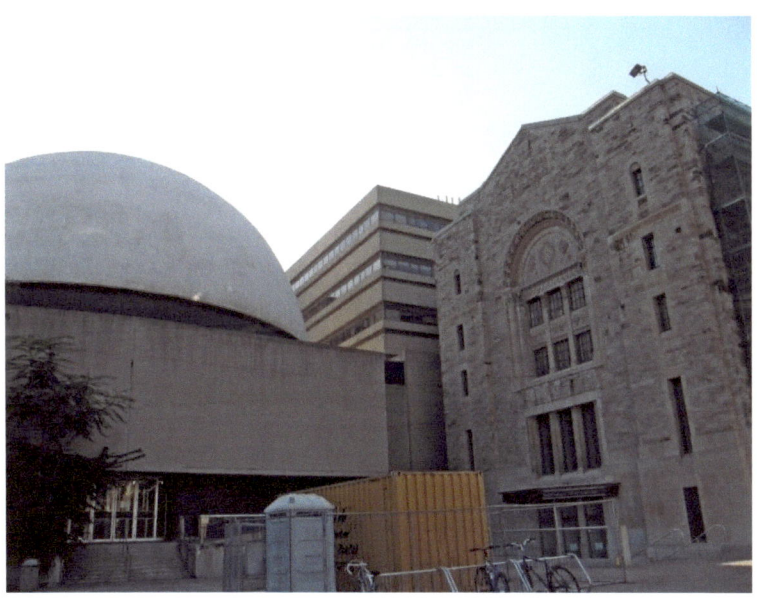

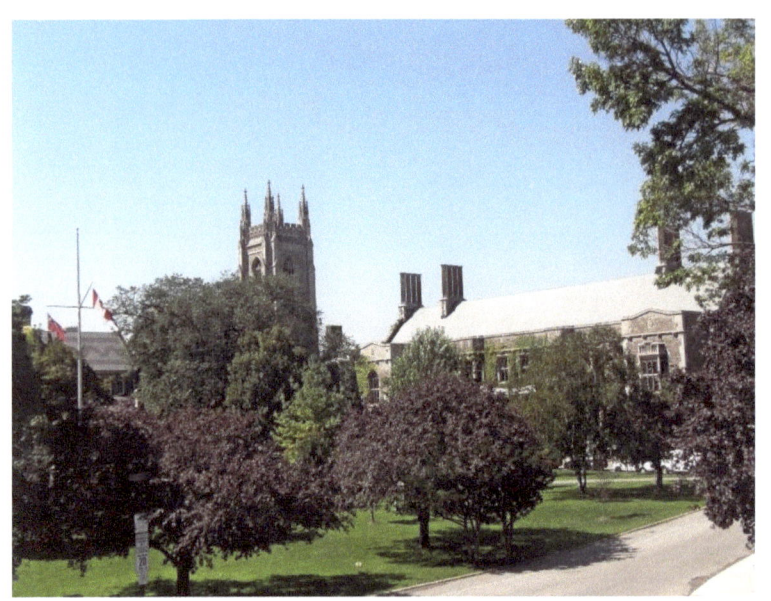
Cathedral

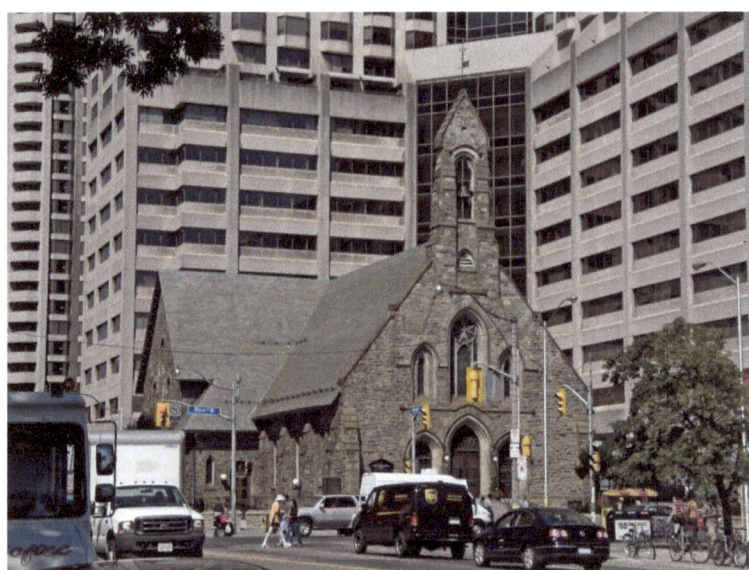
Old church at Bloor Street

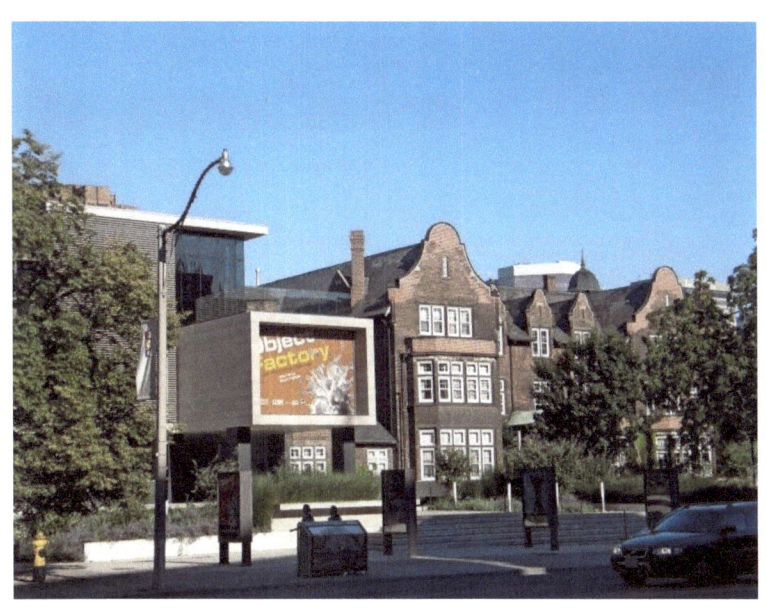

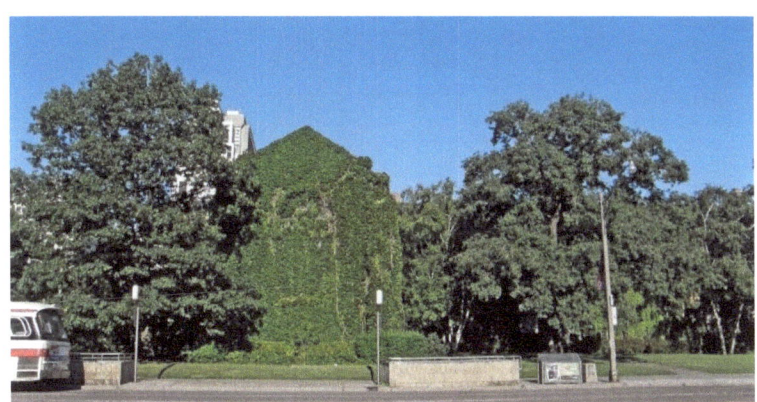

Vine covered building

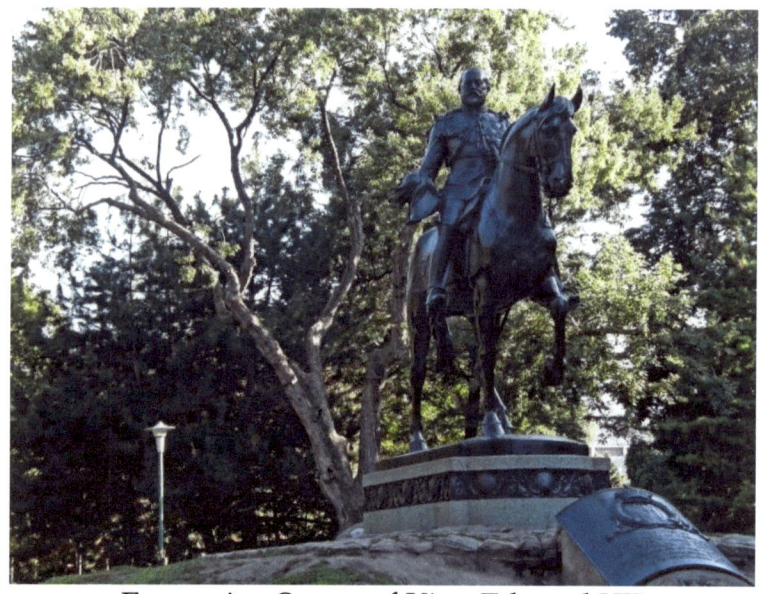

Equestrian Statue of King Edward VII

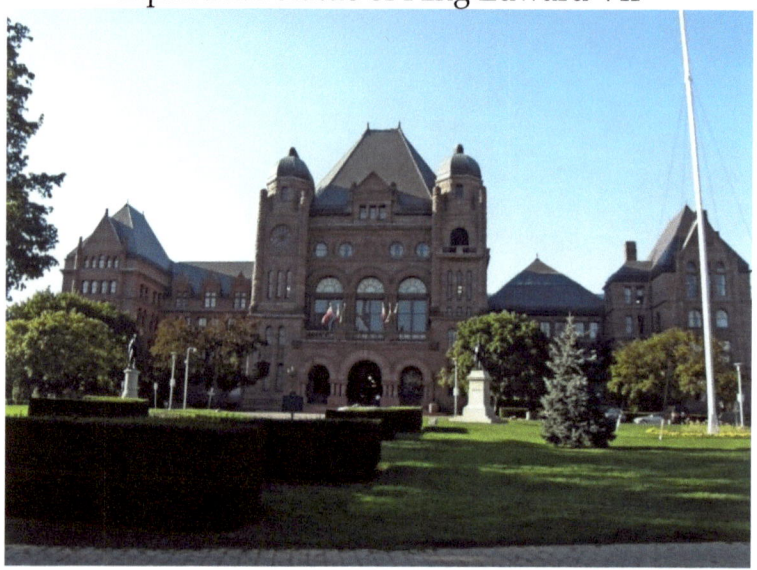

Queen's Park – In 1859 the city leased land from King's College and in 1860 a park named after Queen Victoria was opened by the Prince of Wales. The main block of the massive Romanesque Revival Parliament Buildings with its towering legislative block was completed in 1892.

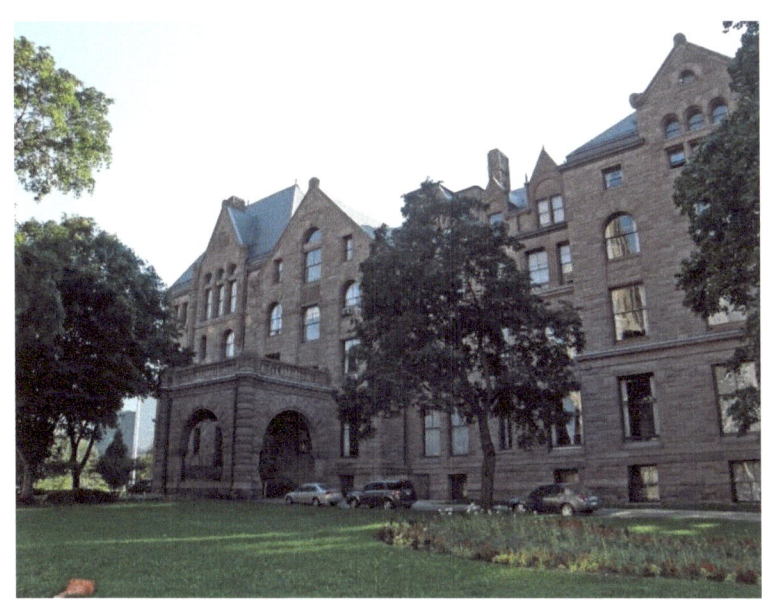

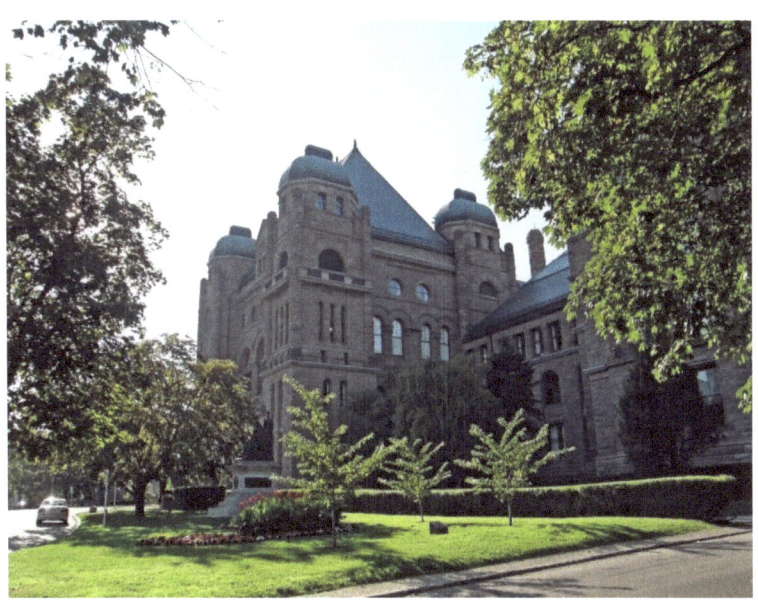

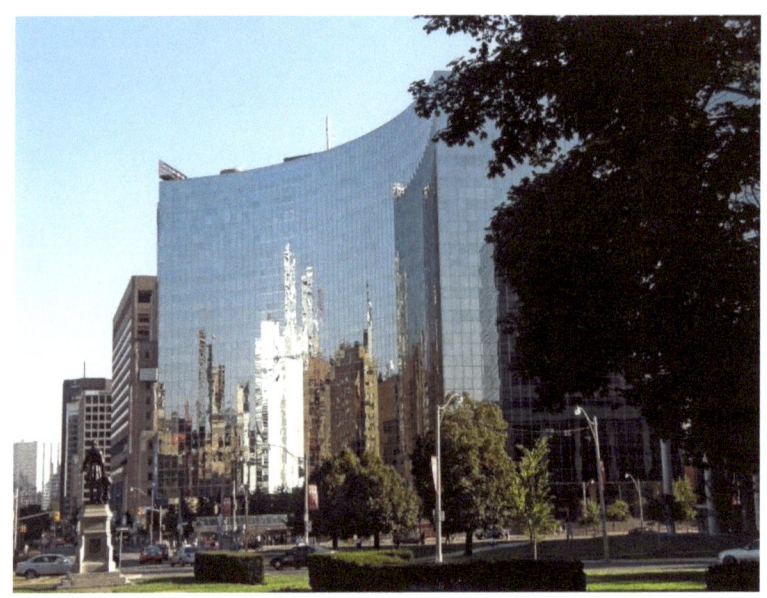
Reflections

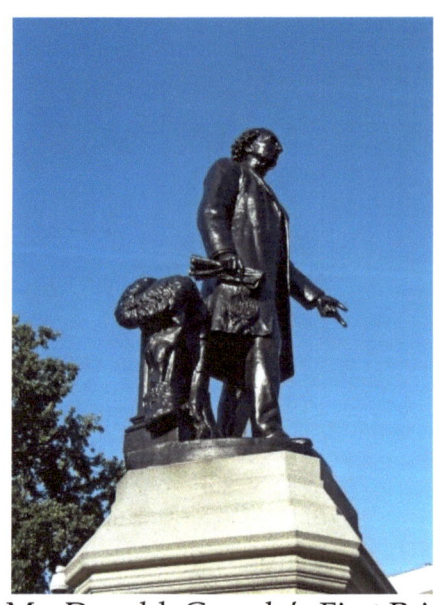
Sir John A. MacDonald, Canada's First Prime Minister

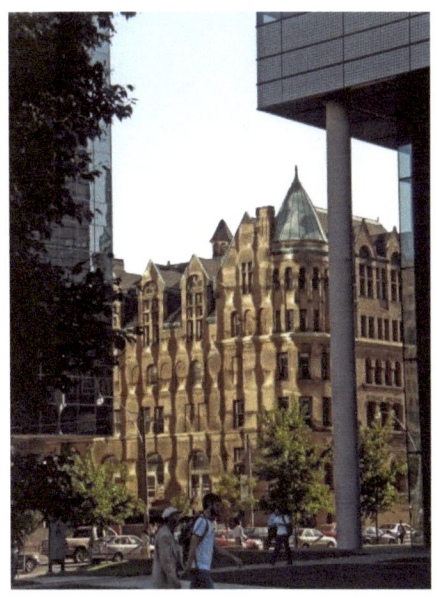
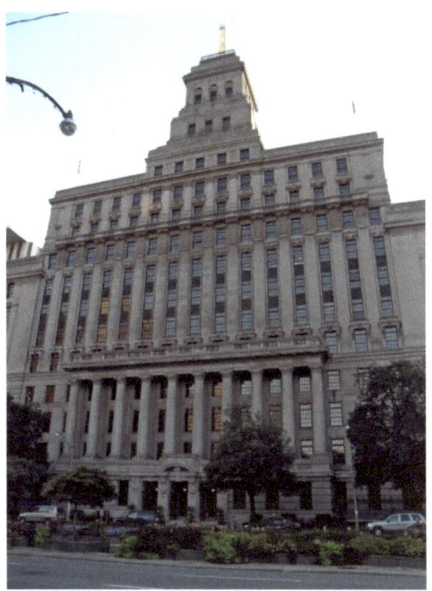
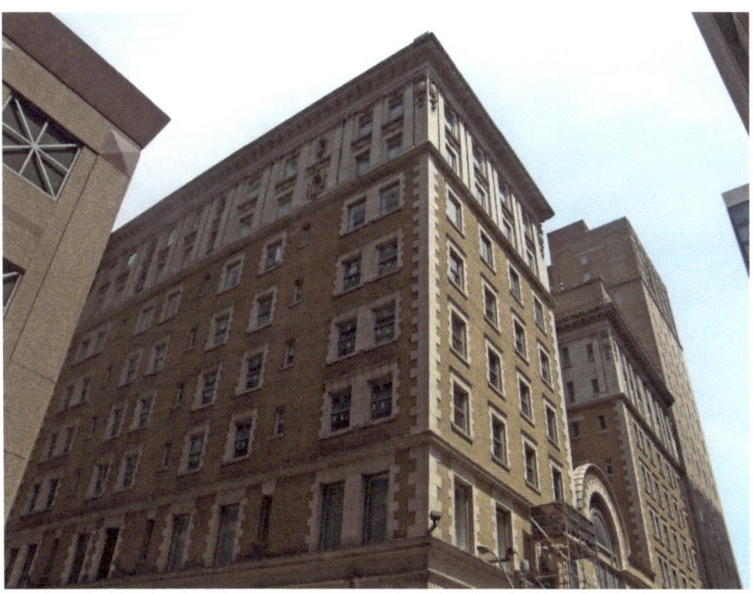

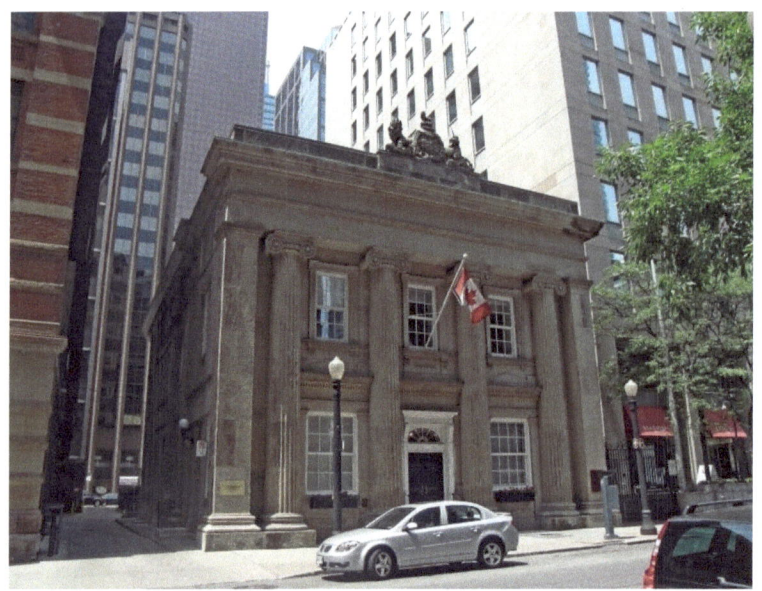

10 Toronto Street – Morgan Meighen & Associates Investment Management

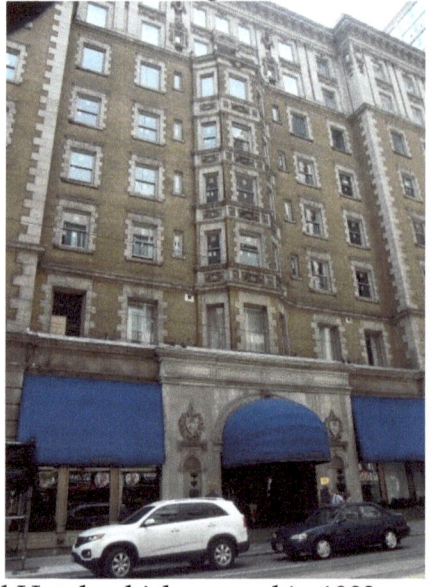

The King Edward Hotel, which opened in 1903, was built to meet the demand in the metropolis for a grand hotel. The fireproof, eight-storey building provided luxury and service. The eighteen-storey tower with its top-floor Crystal Ballroom was added in 1920-21 to enlarge the hotel.

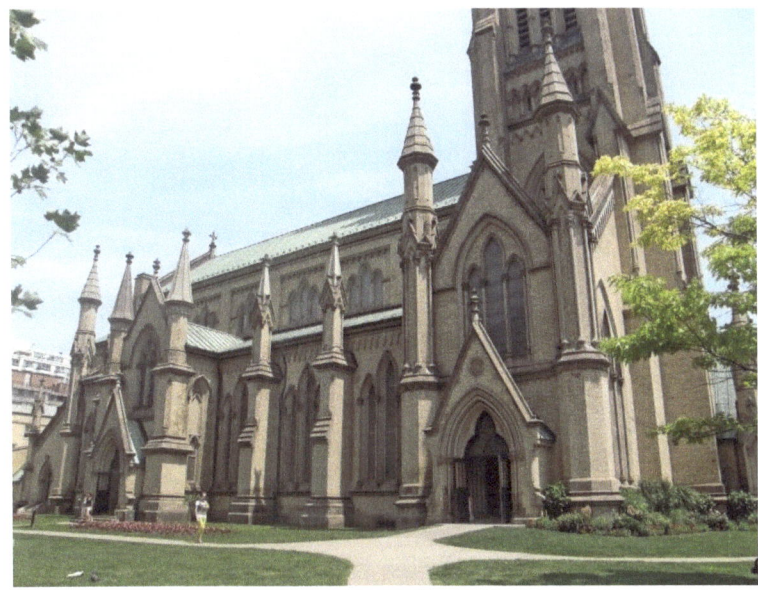

The first church in York was a frame building built in 1803-07; it was replaced by a larger one in 1831 which was destroyed by fire in 1839. The first cathedral was erected on this site but was destroyed in the great fire of 1849. The present cathedral was begun in 1850 and opened in 1853.

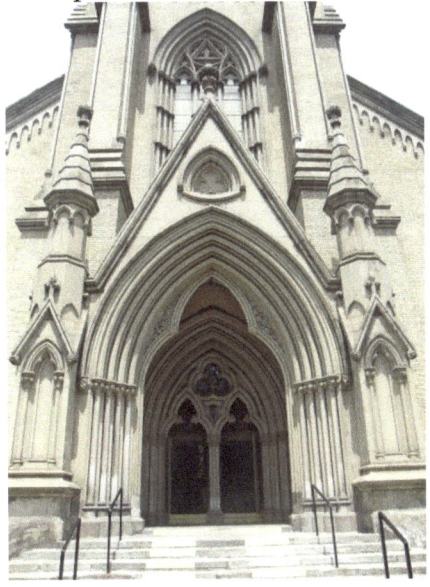
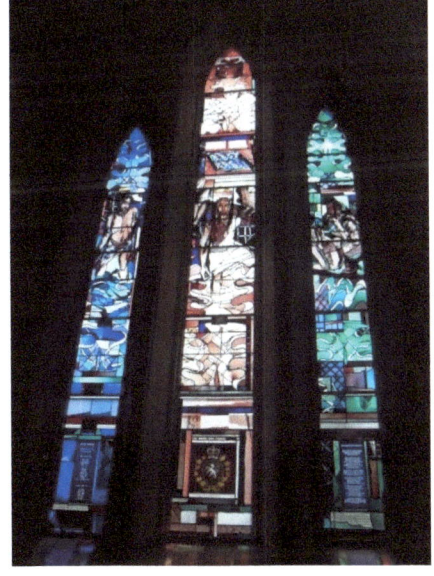

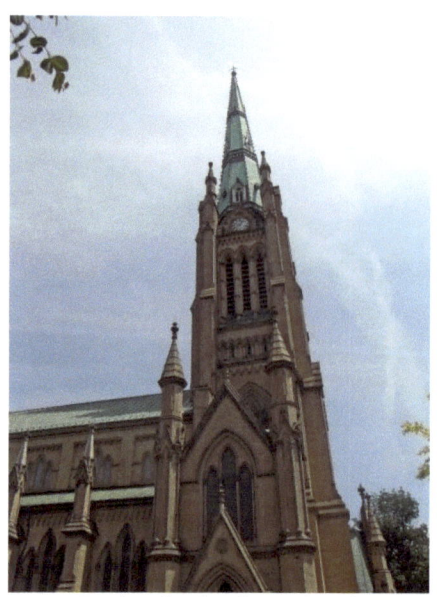

65 Church Street – Cathedral Church of St. James, Anglican

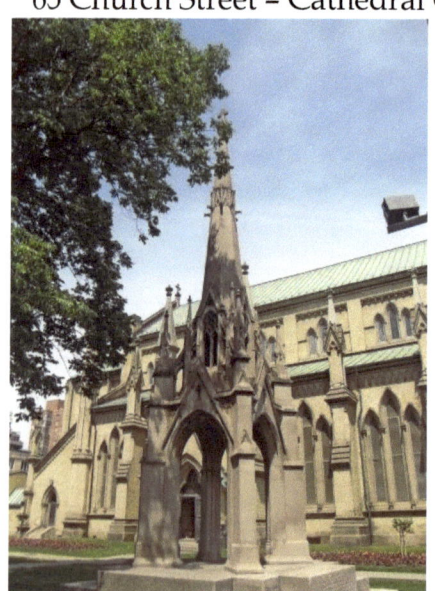
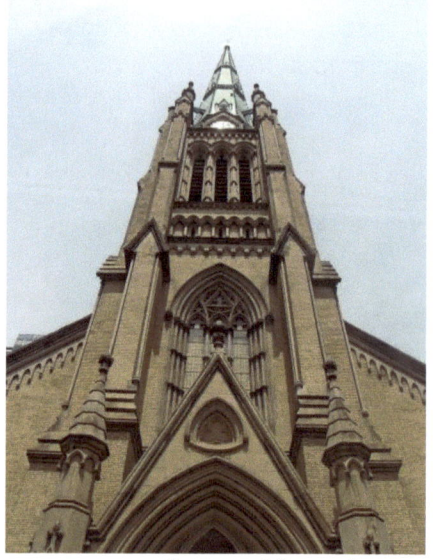

The James Cathedral cross commemorates the sacrifice of those who gave their lives in World War I.

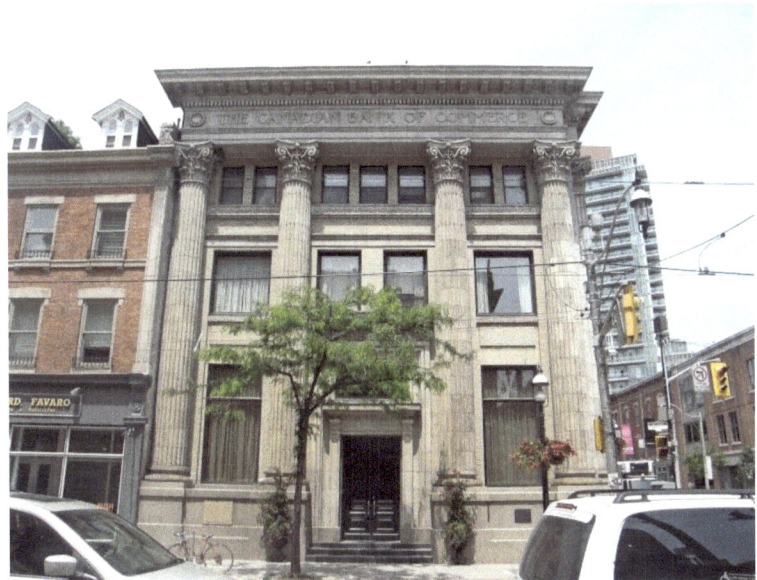

The Canadian Bank of Commerce

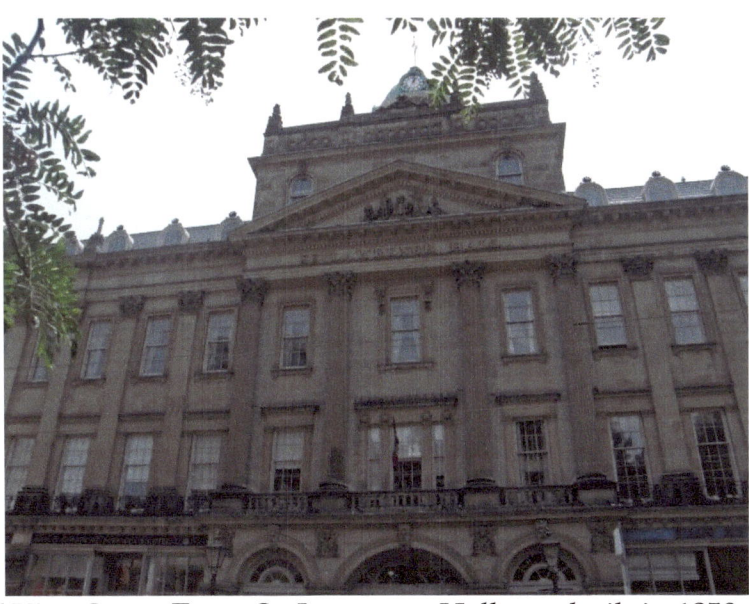

157 King Street East - St. Lawrence Hall was built in 1850 and restored to its original grandeur in 1967. It was created to be Toronto's public meeting hall for public gatherings, concerts, and exhibitions.

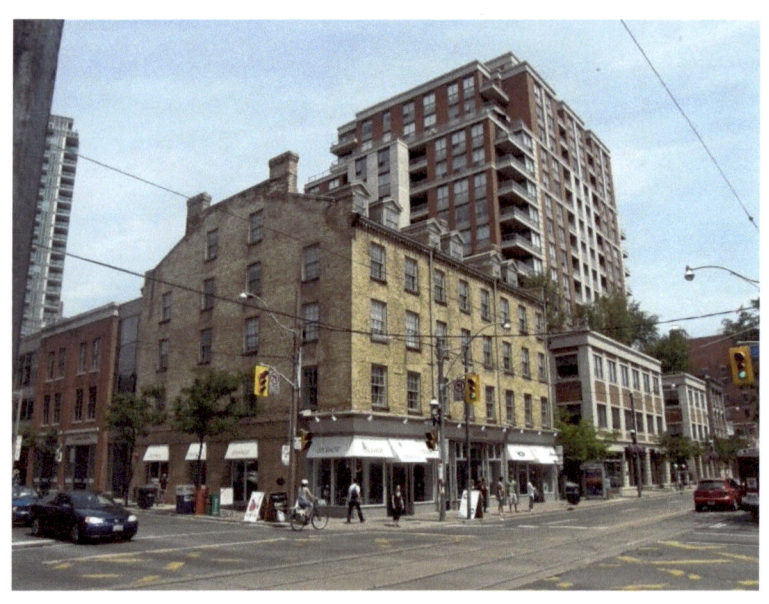

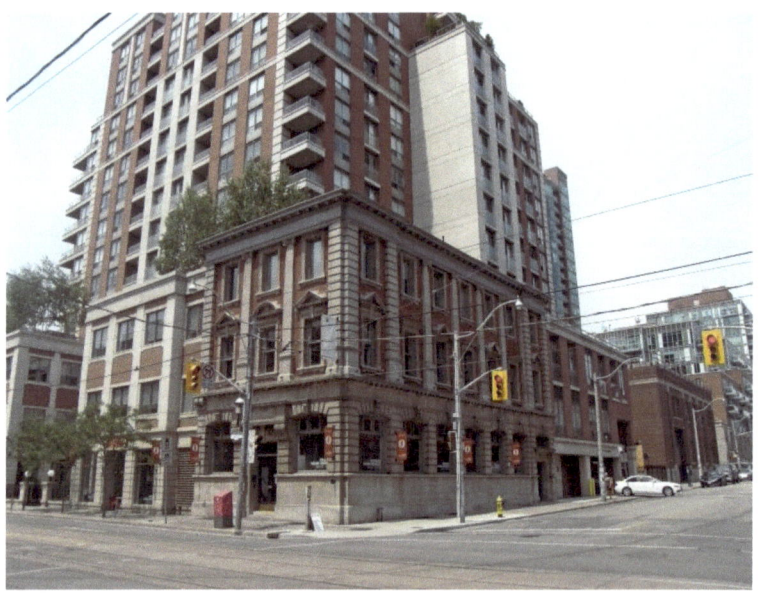

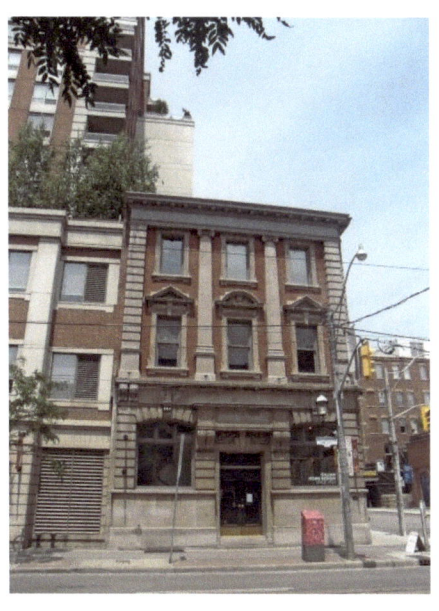

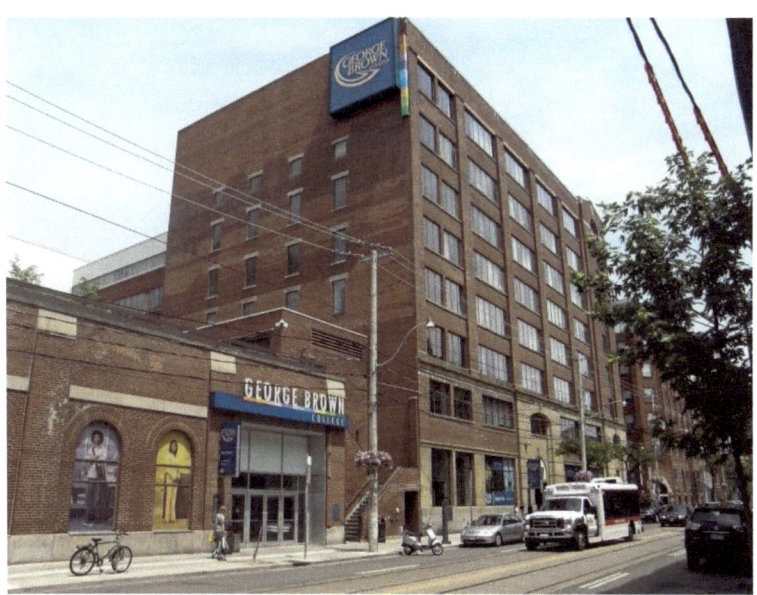

George Brown College

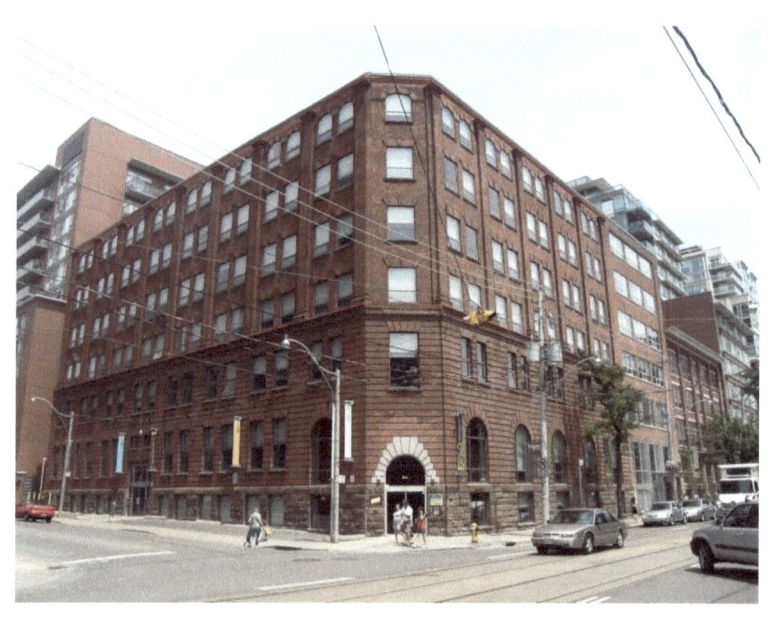

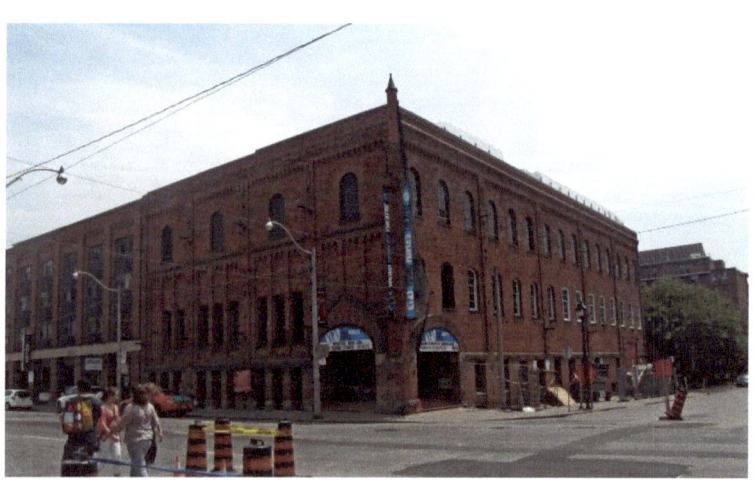

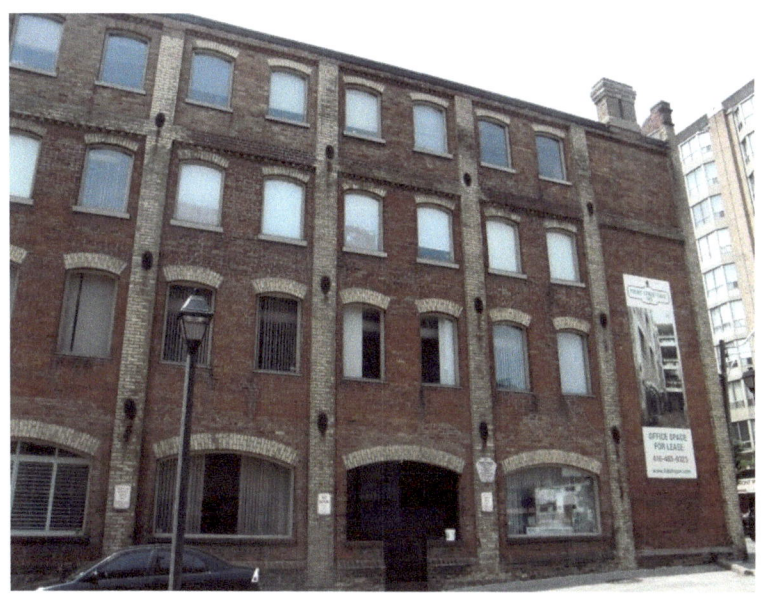

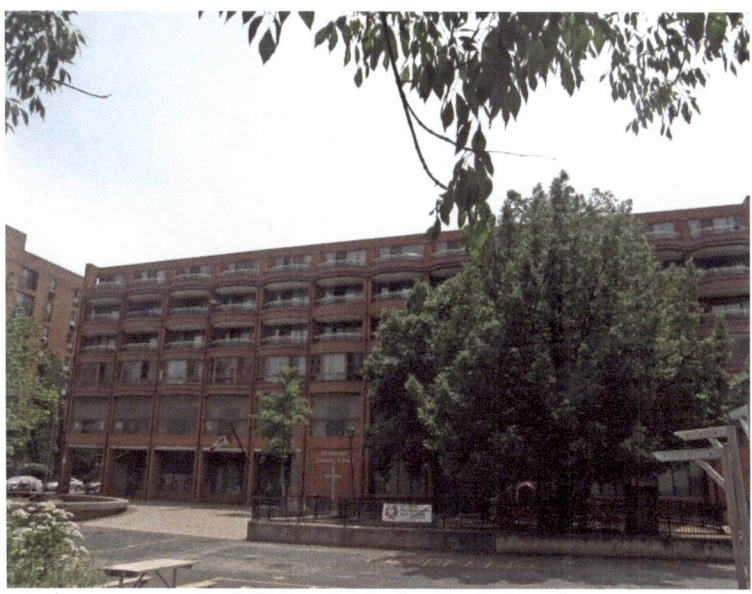

St. Michael Catholic School

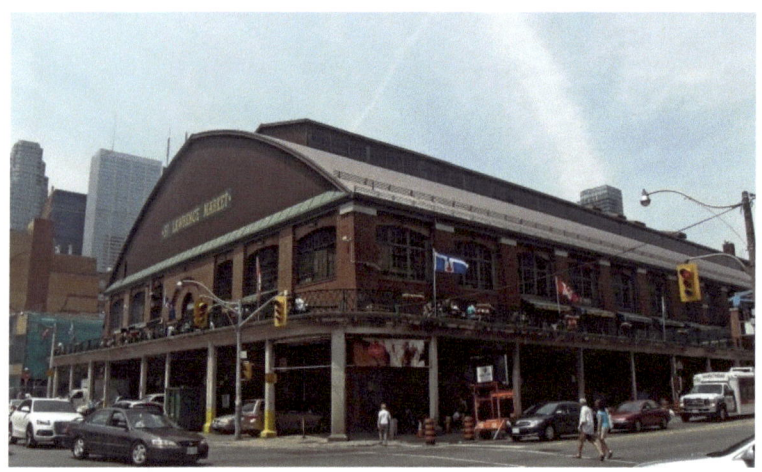

St. Lawrence Market

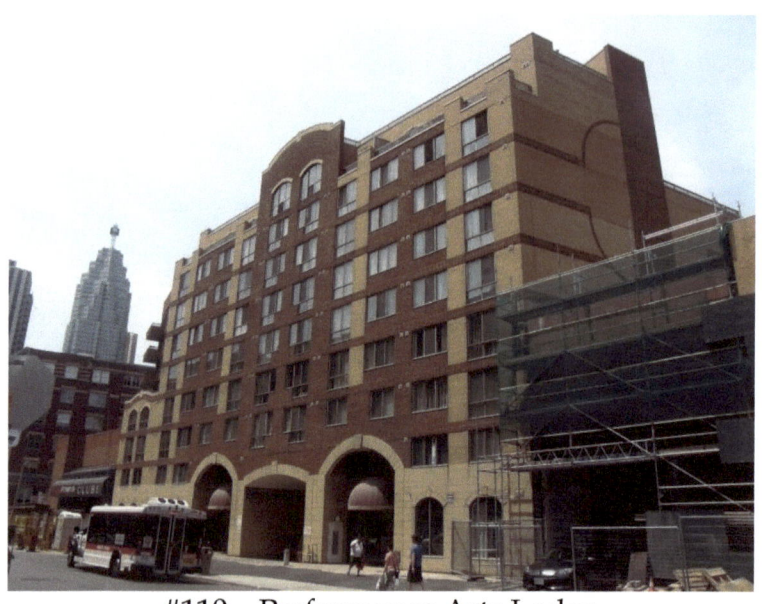

#110 – Performance Arts Lodge

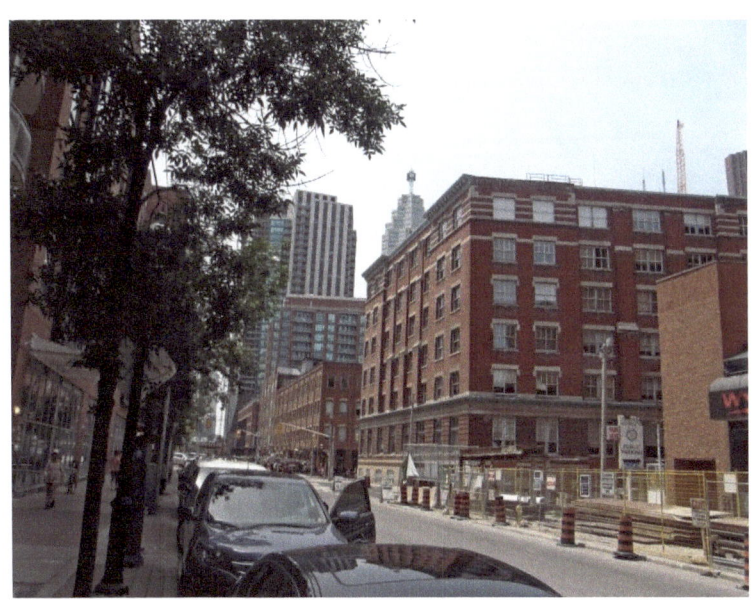

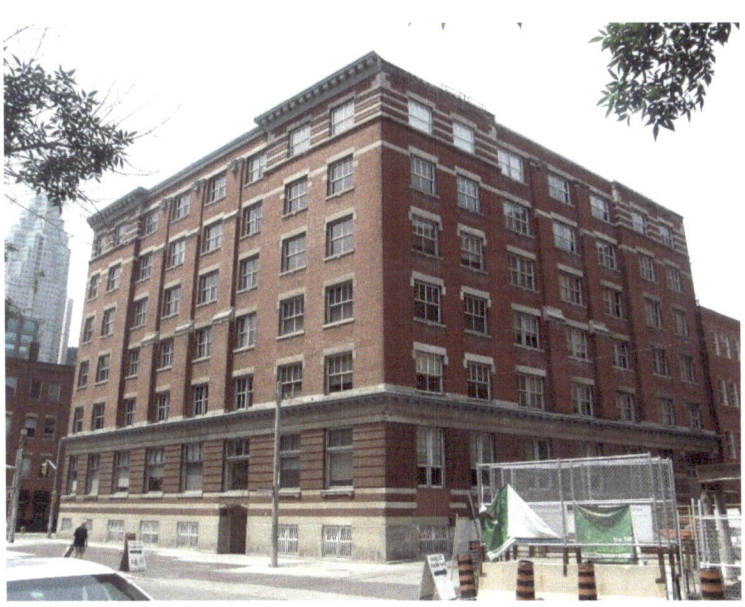

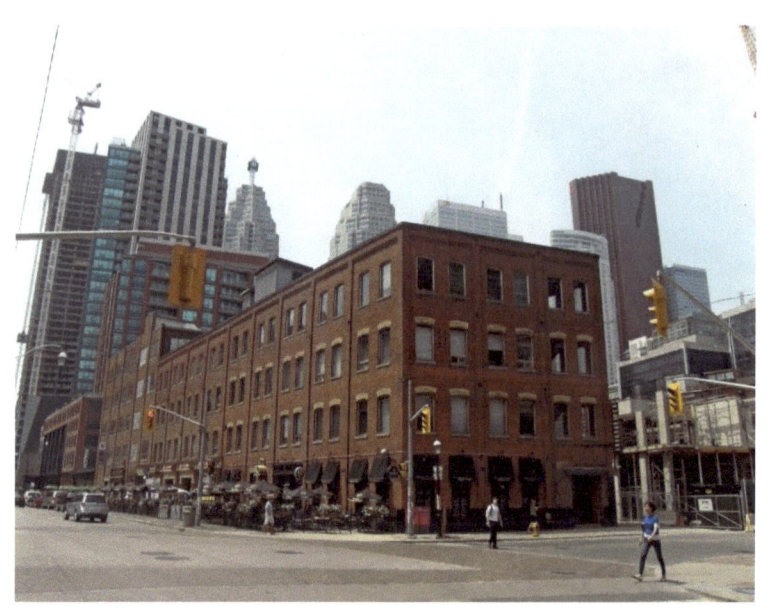

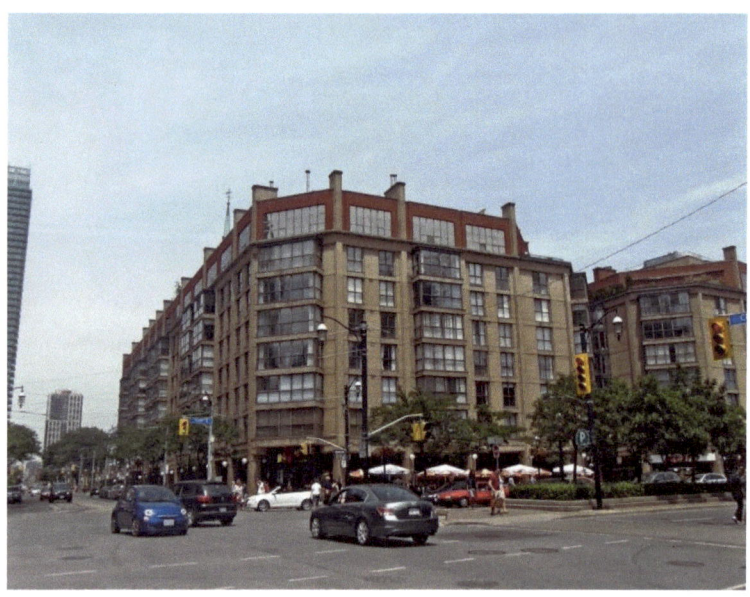

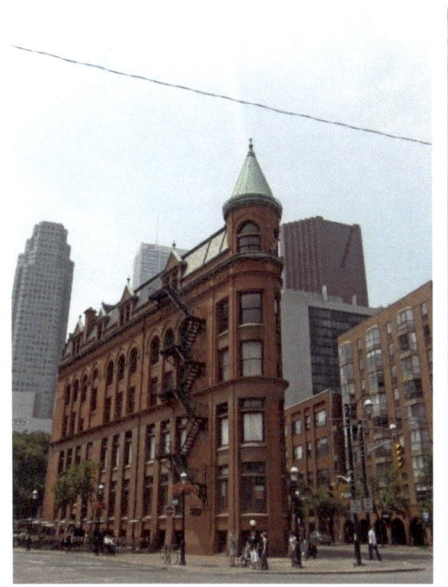
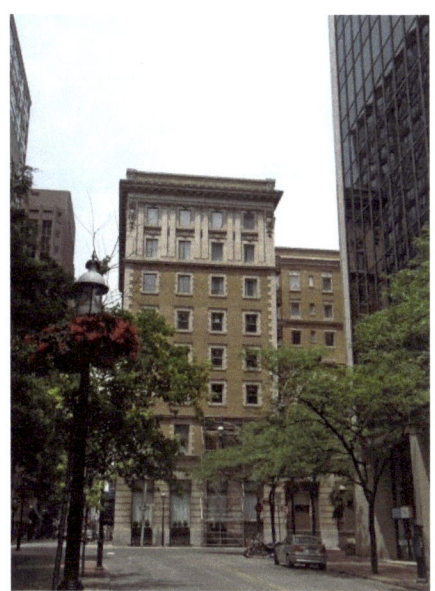

49 Wellington Street East
The Gooderham or Flatiron Building
Romanesque Revival and French Gothic architecture styles
Opened in 1892

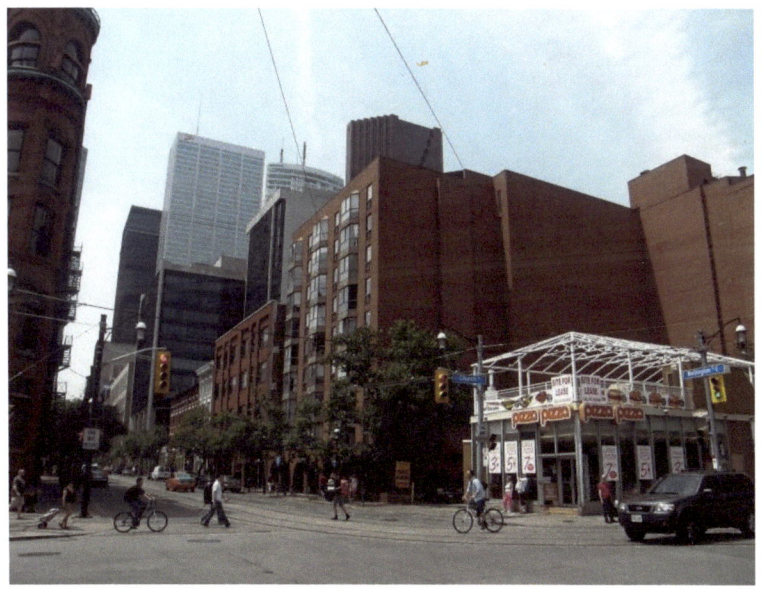

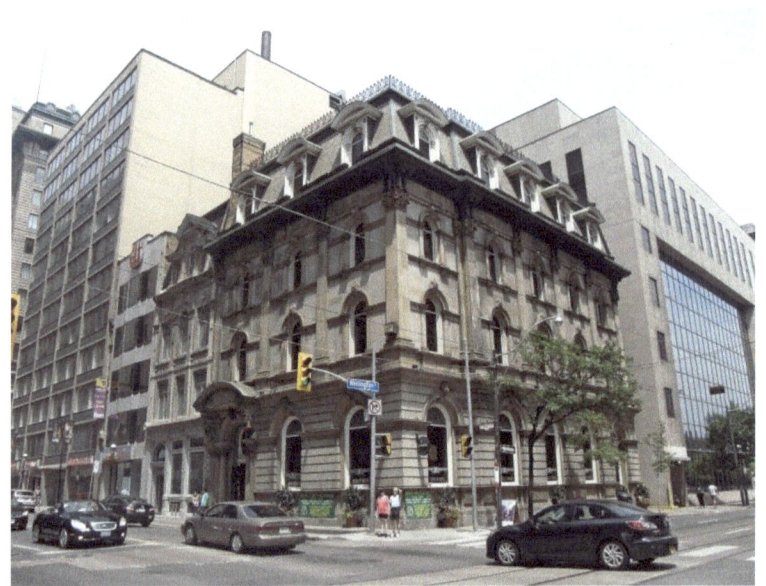
British Colonial Building – 49 Yonge Street at Wellington

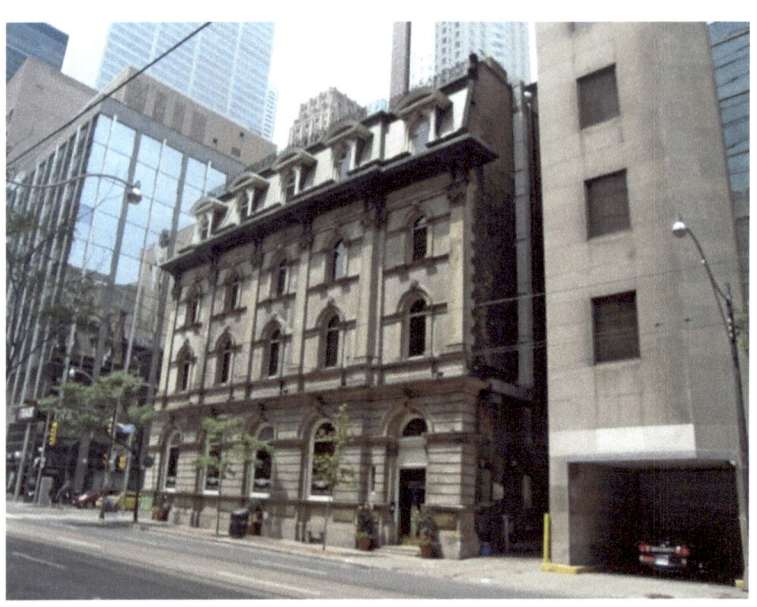

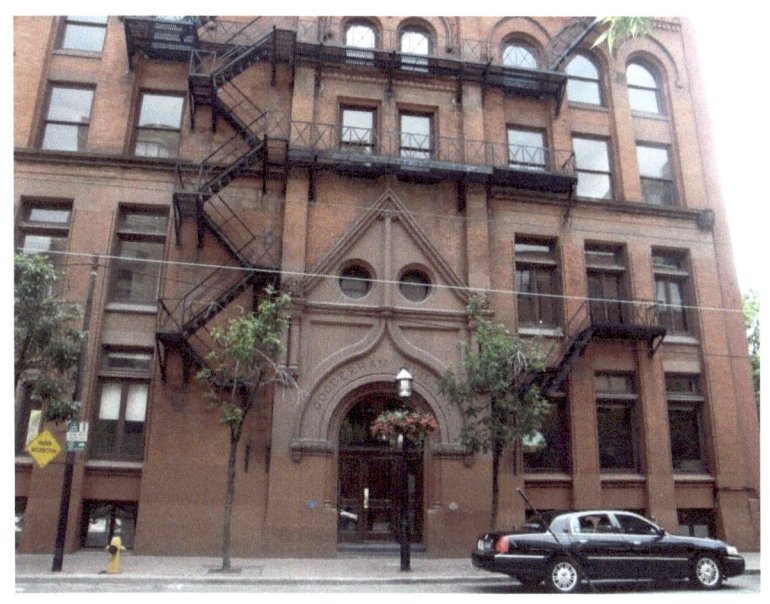

Gooderham Building – 49 Wellington Street East

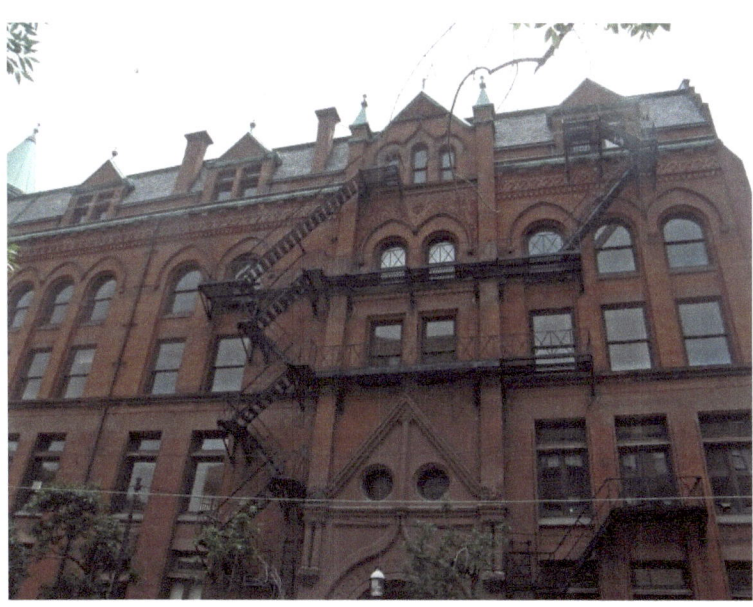

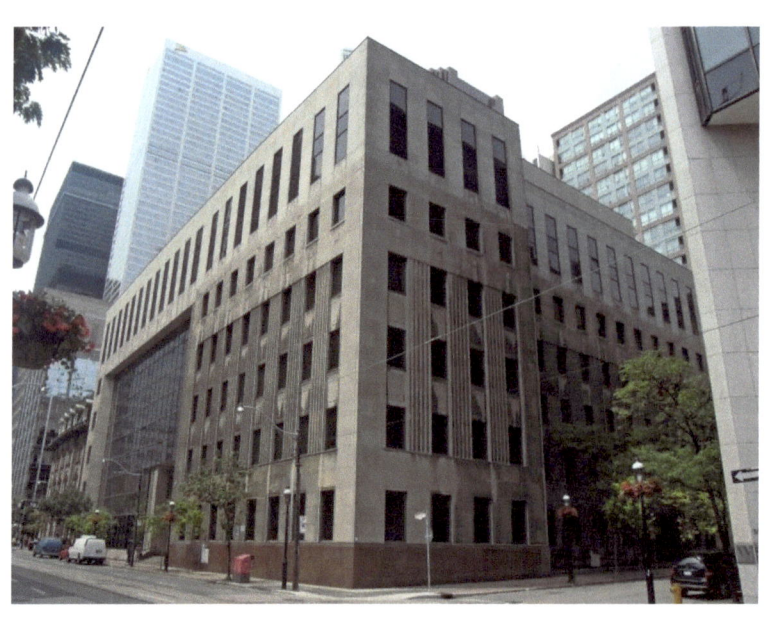

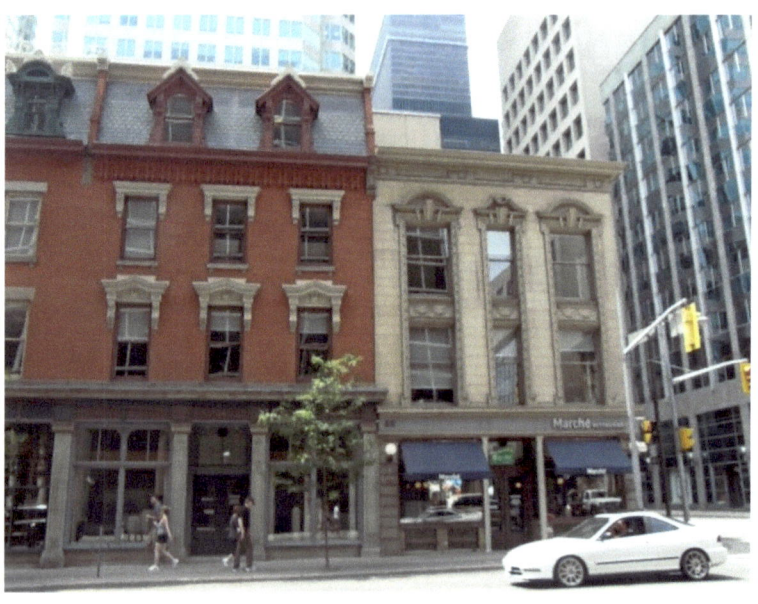

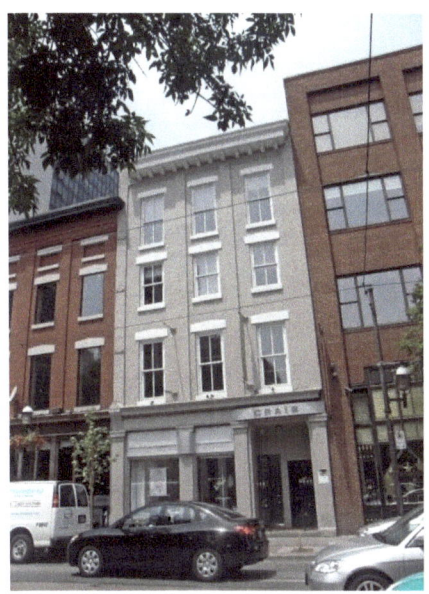
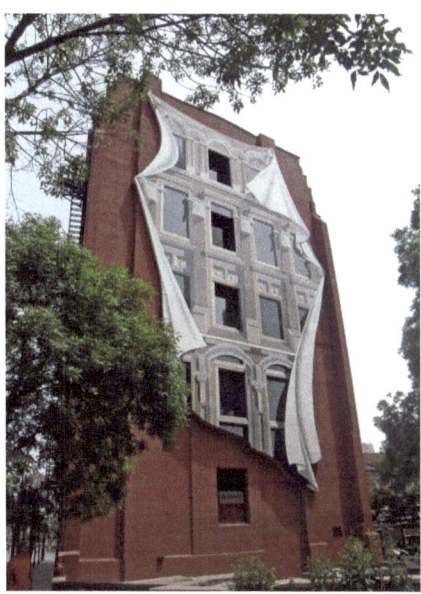
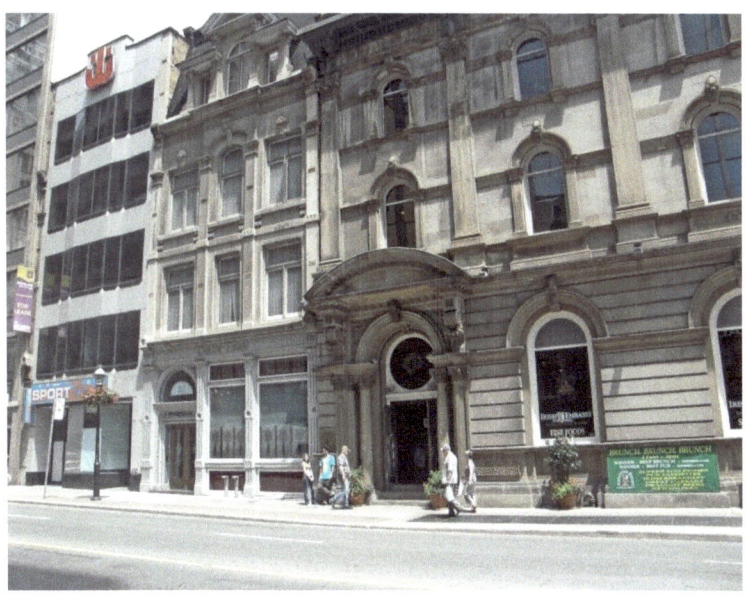

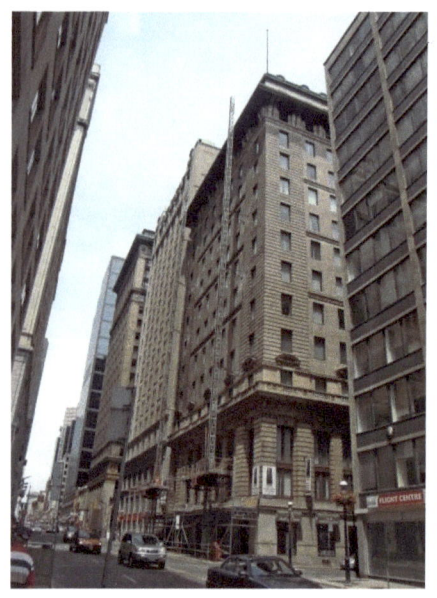 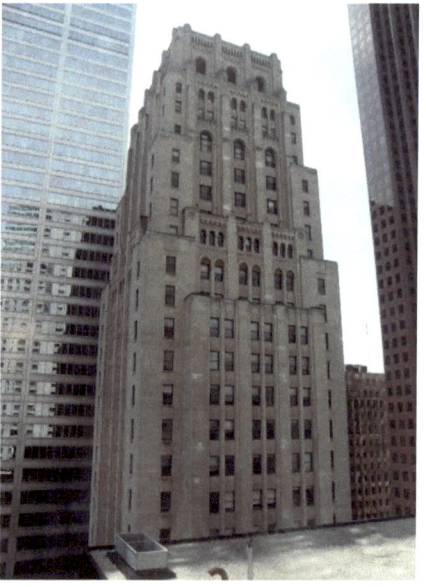

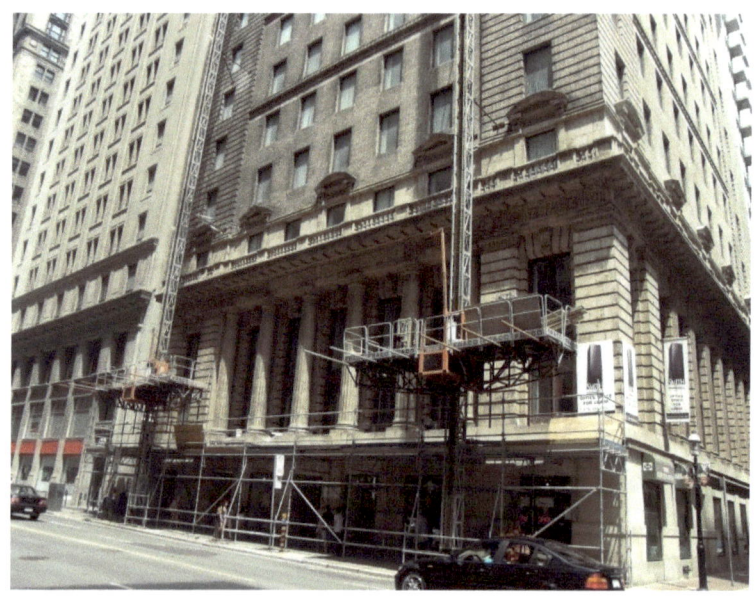

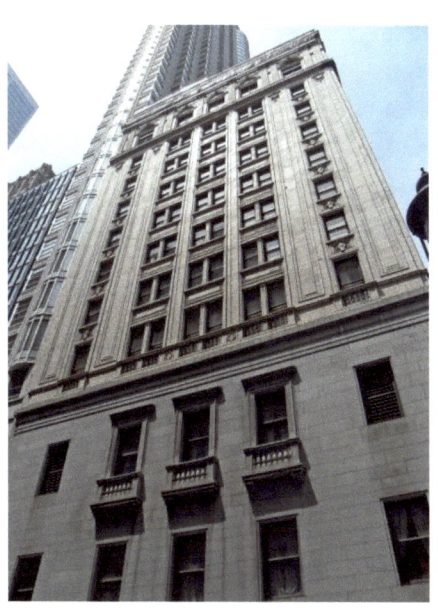

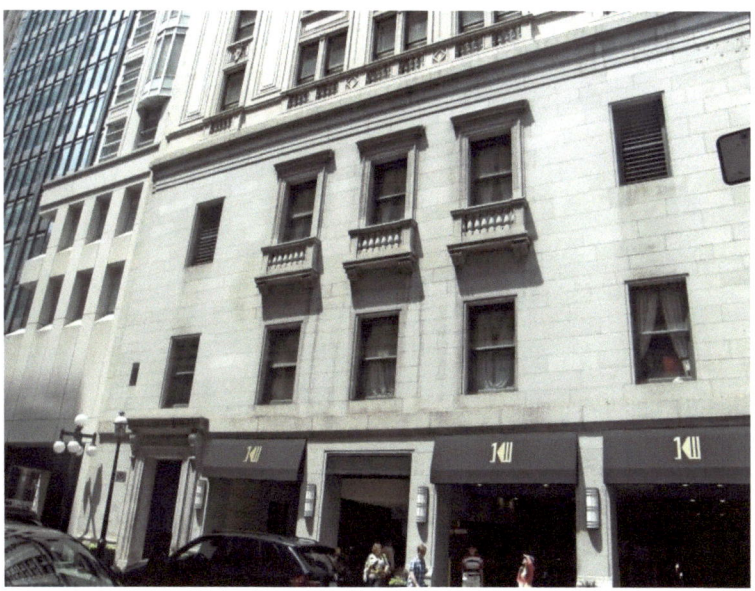

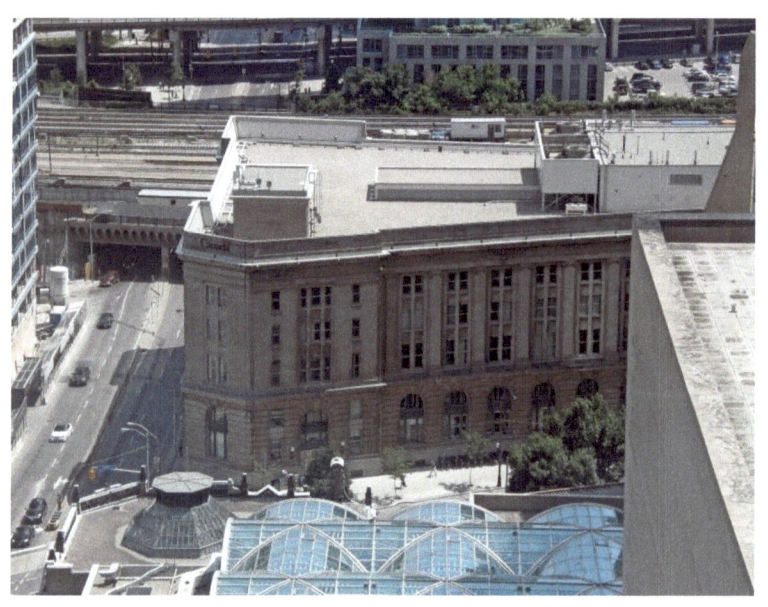

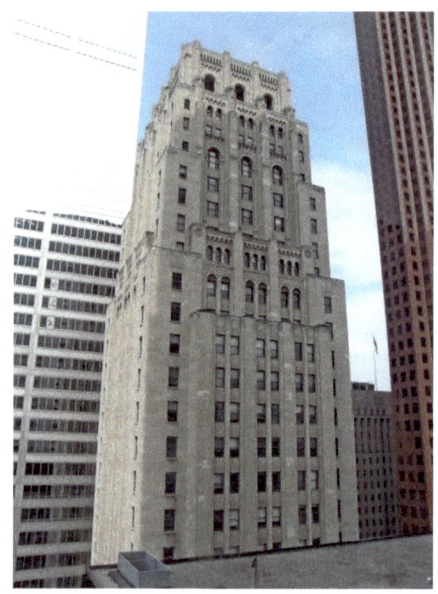

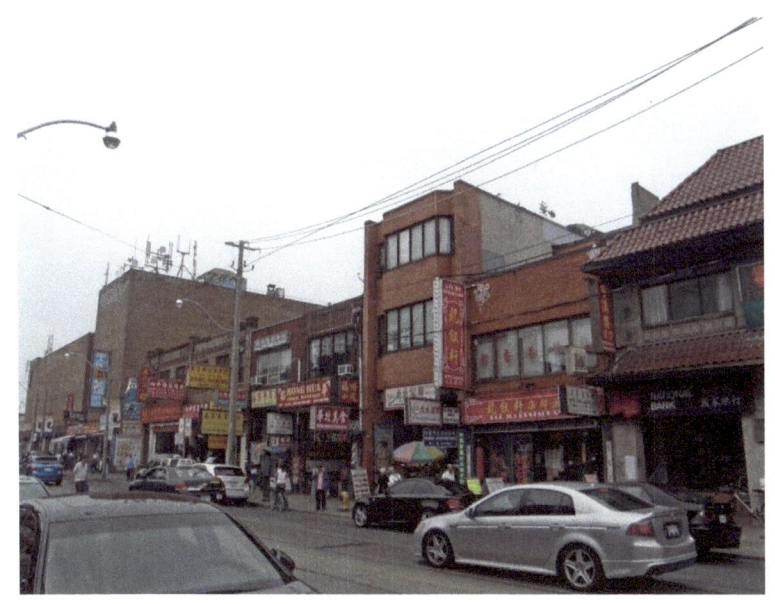

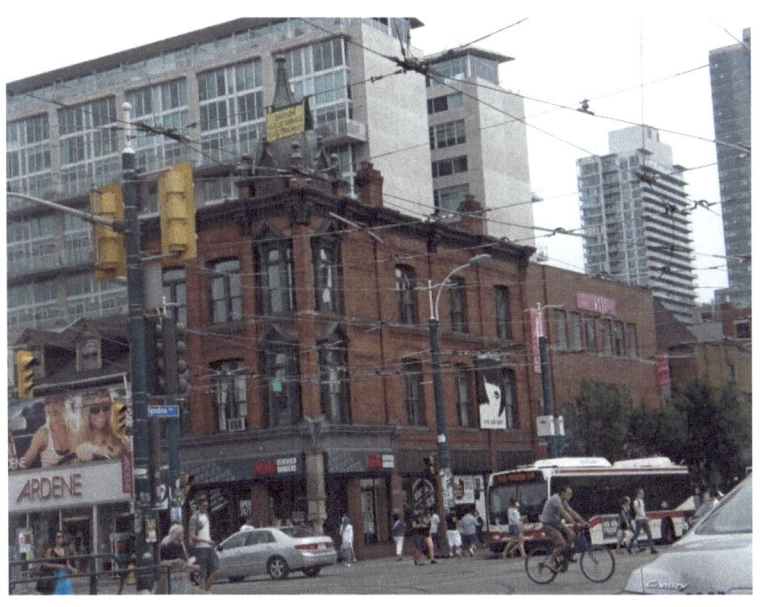

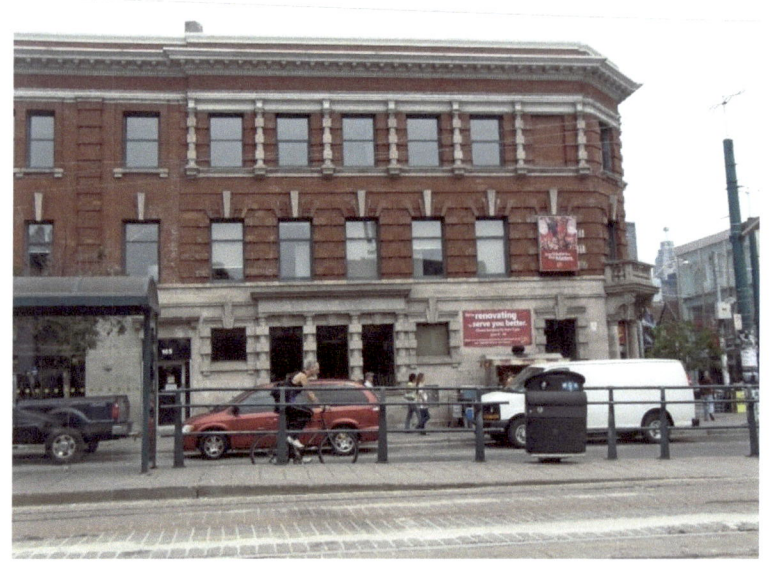

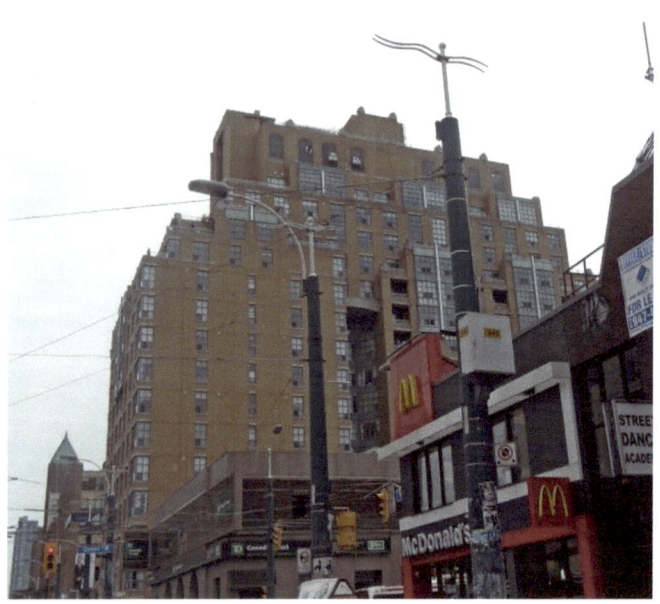

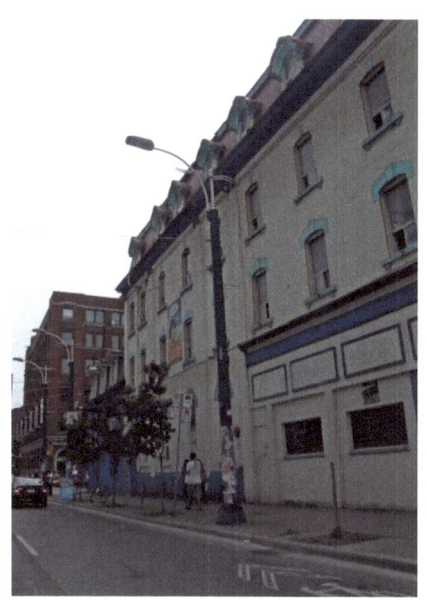
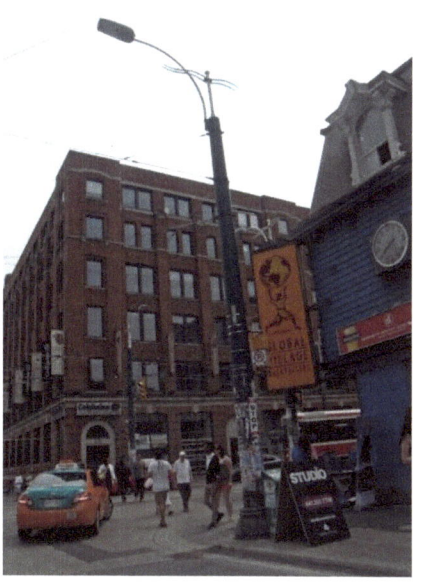
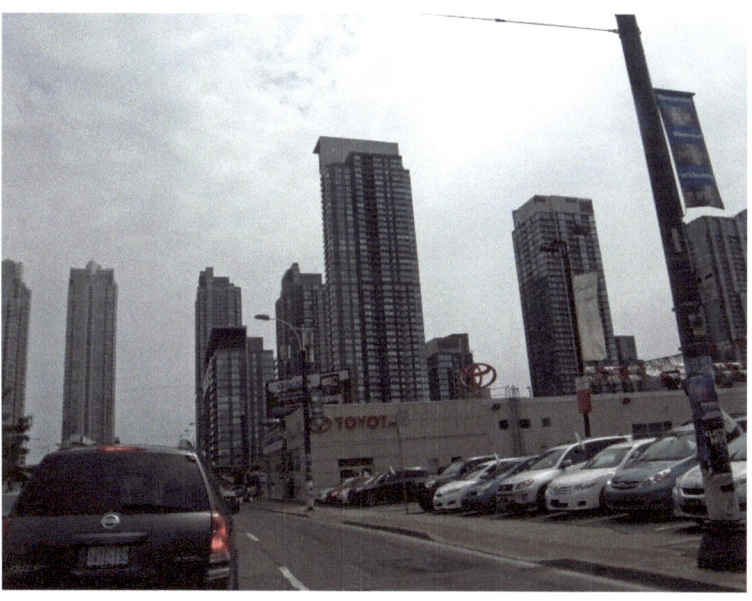

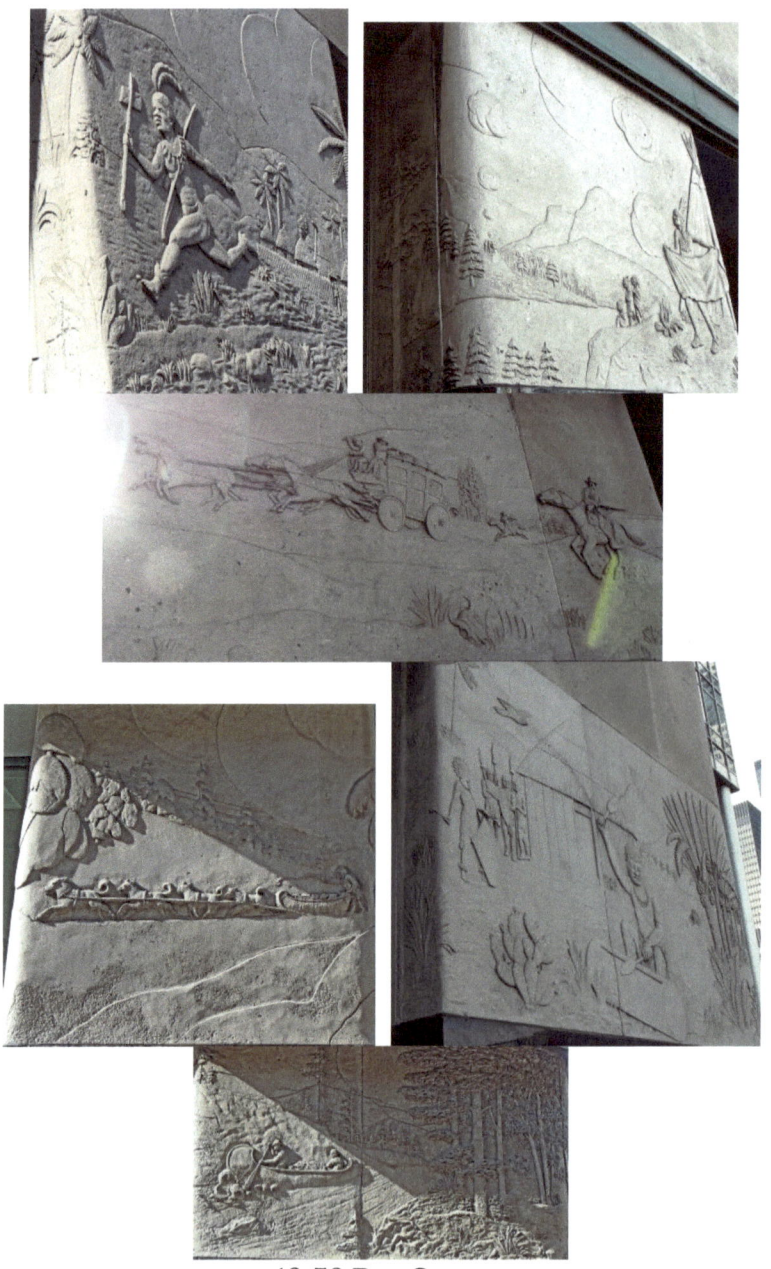

40-50 Bay Street

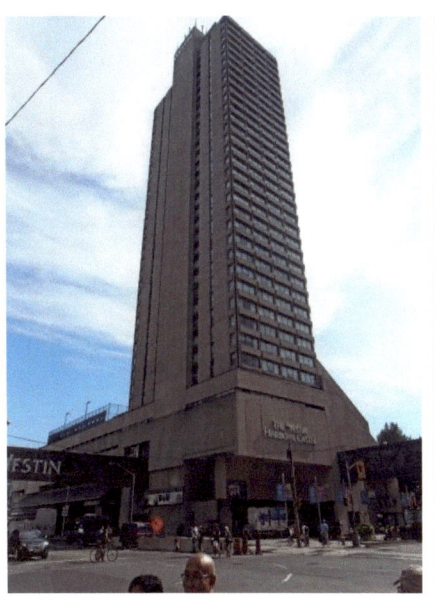
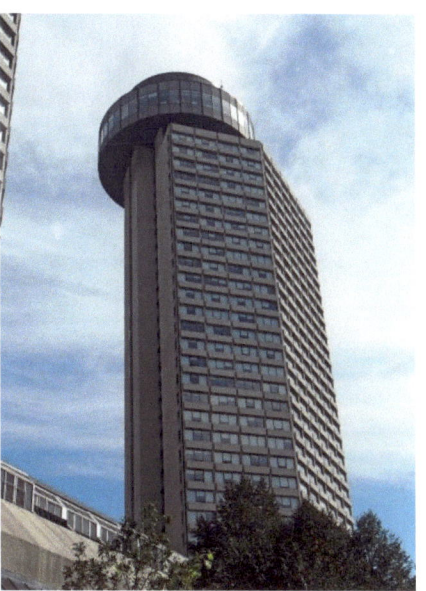
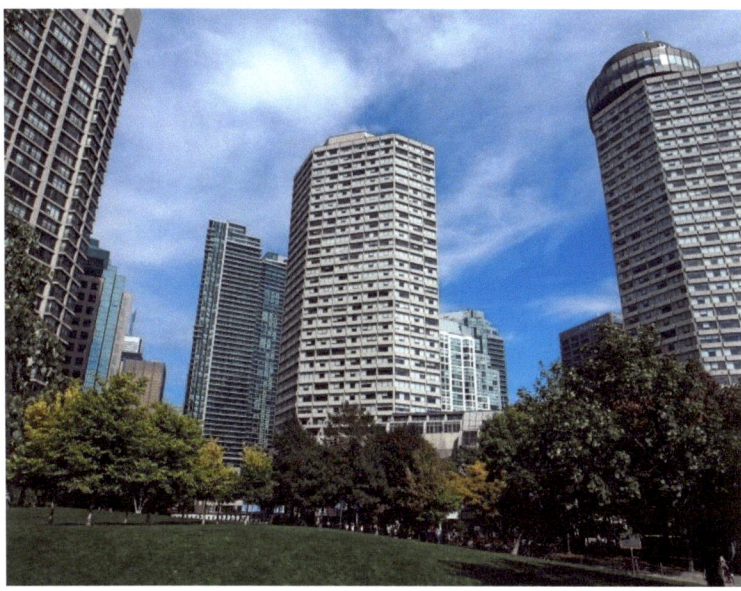

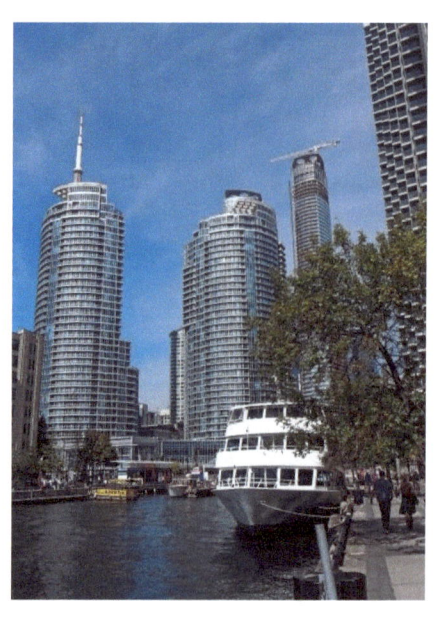

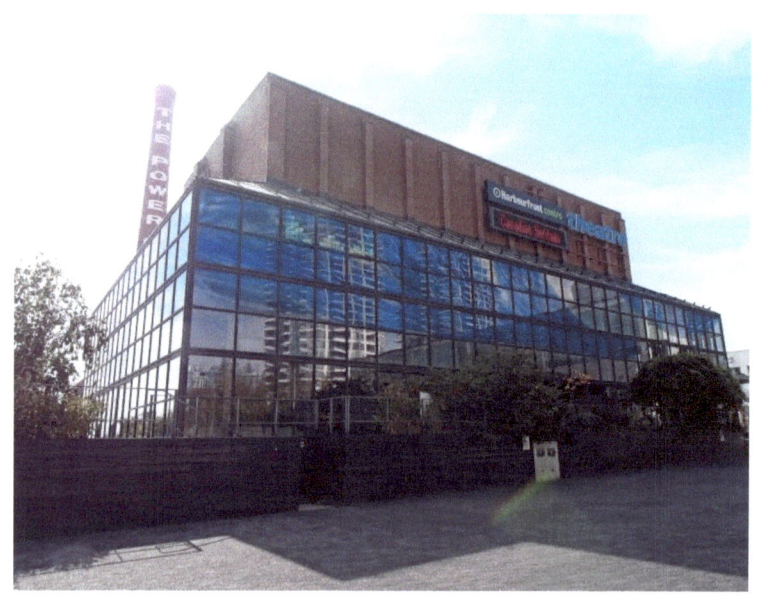

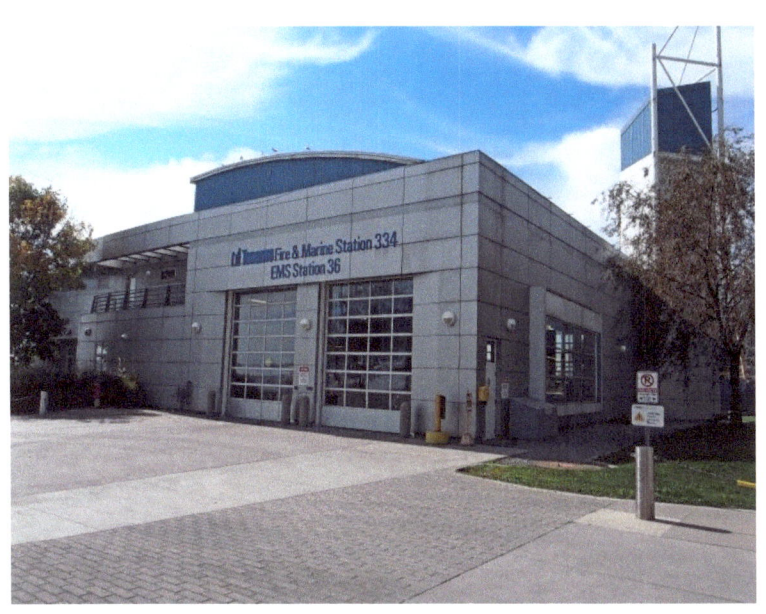

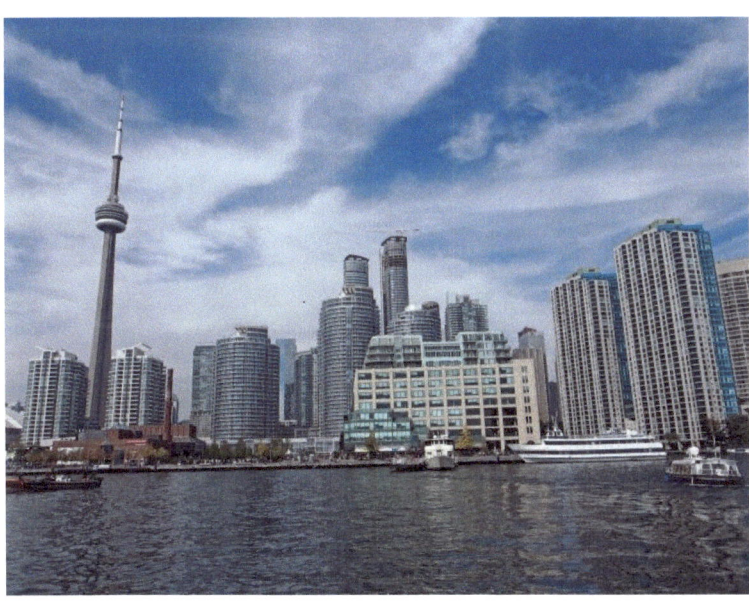

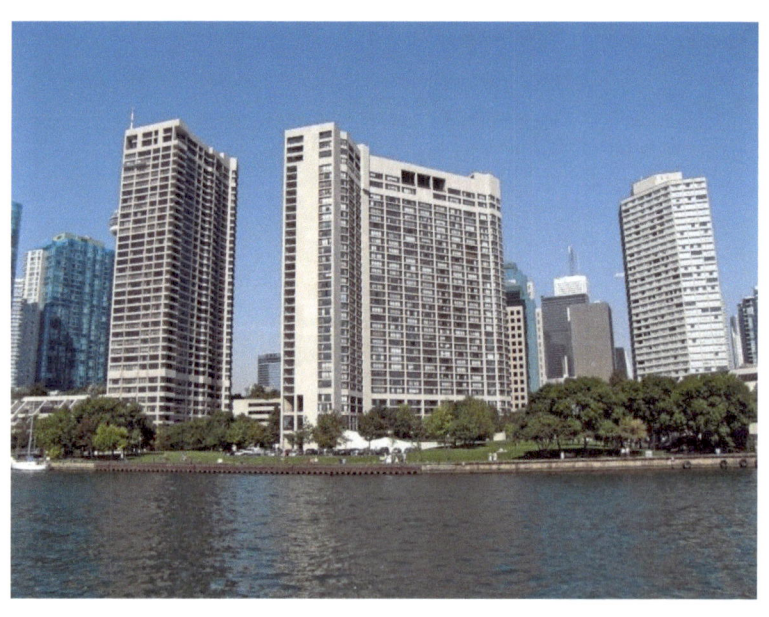

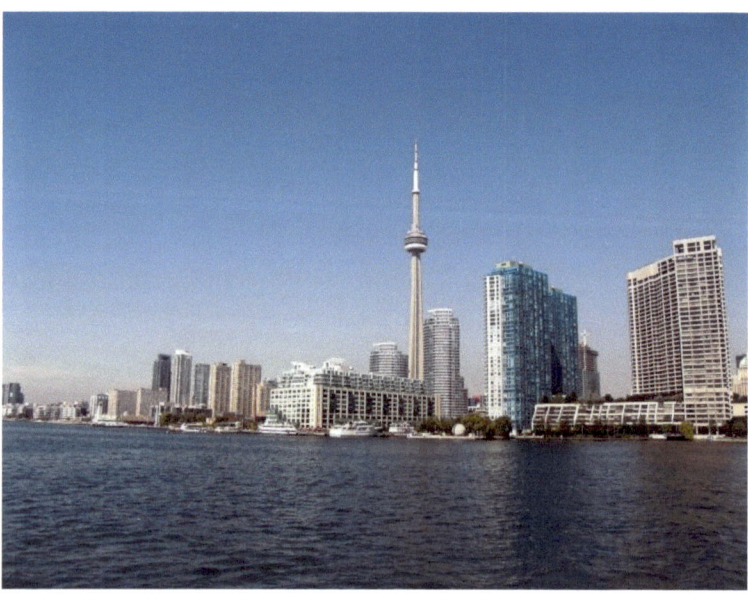

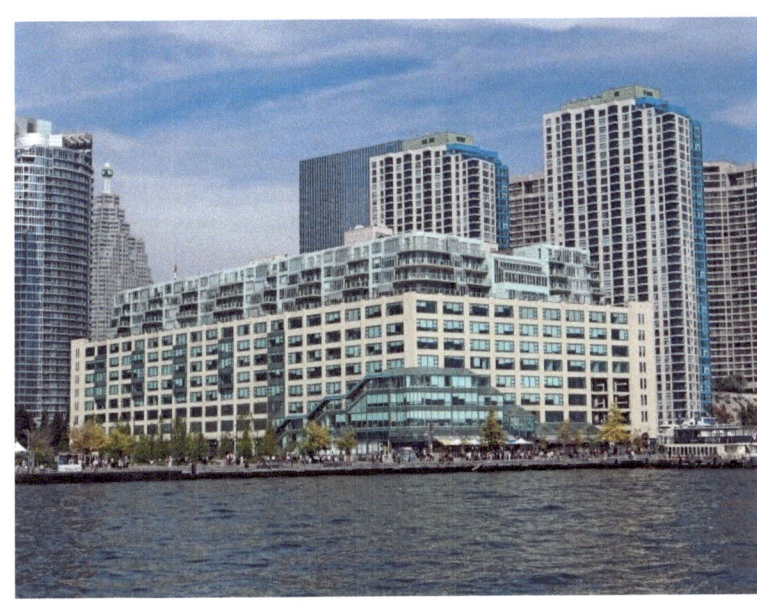

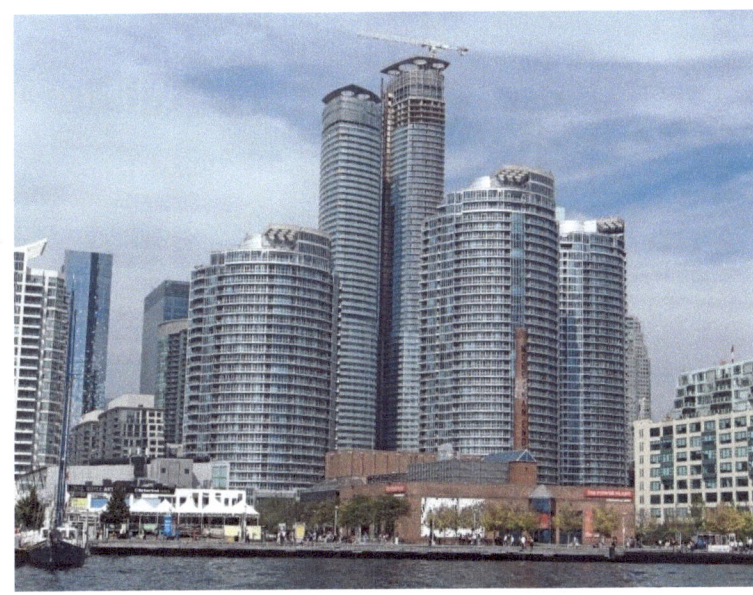

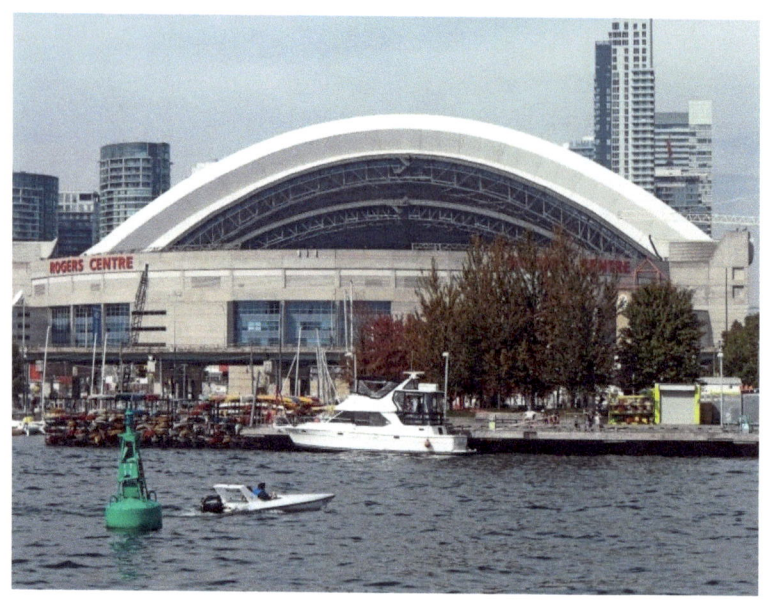

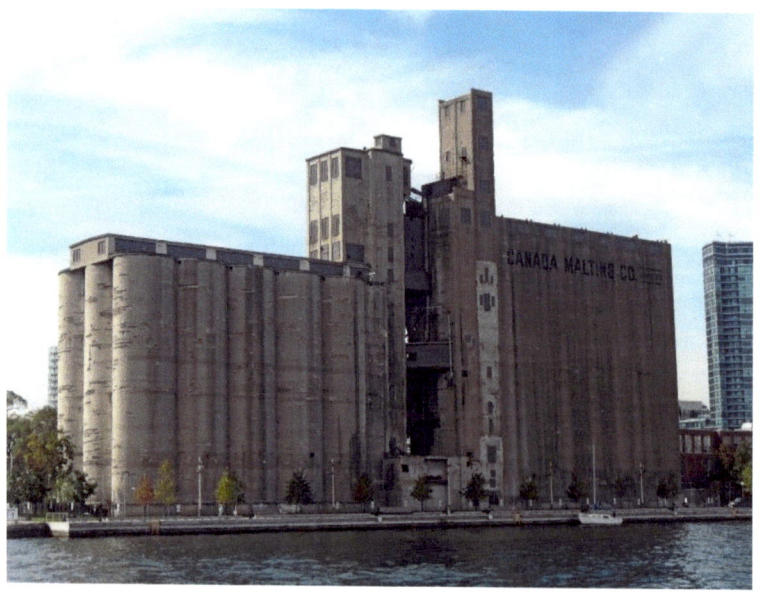

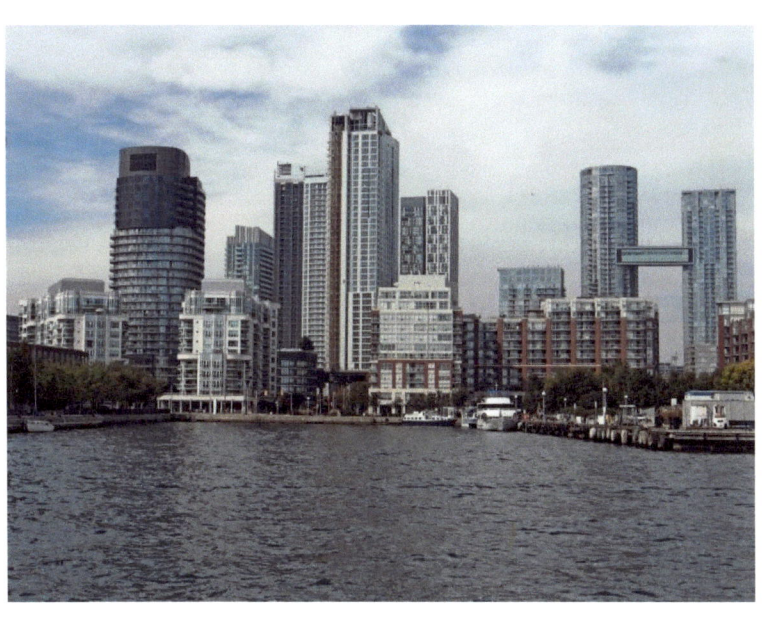

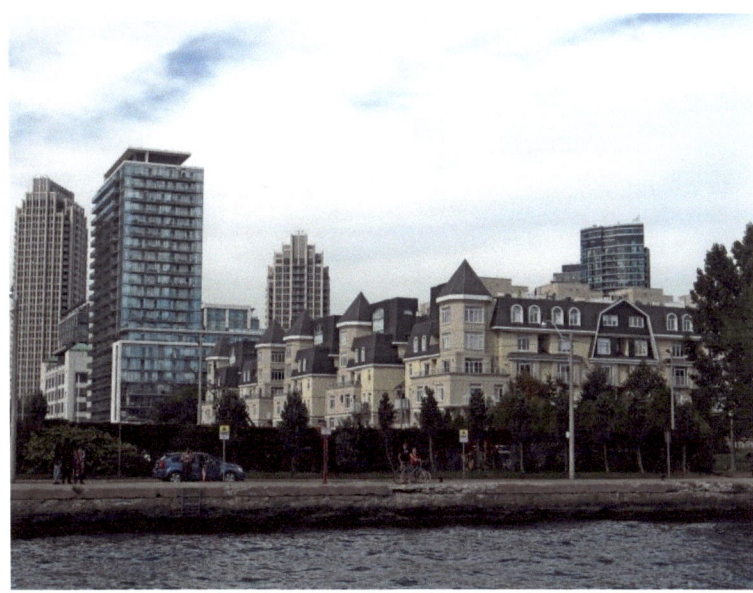

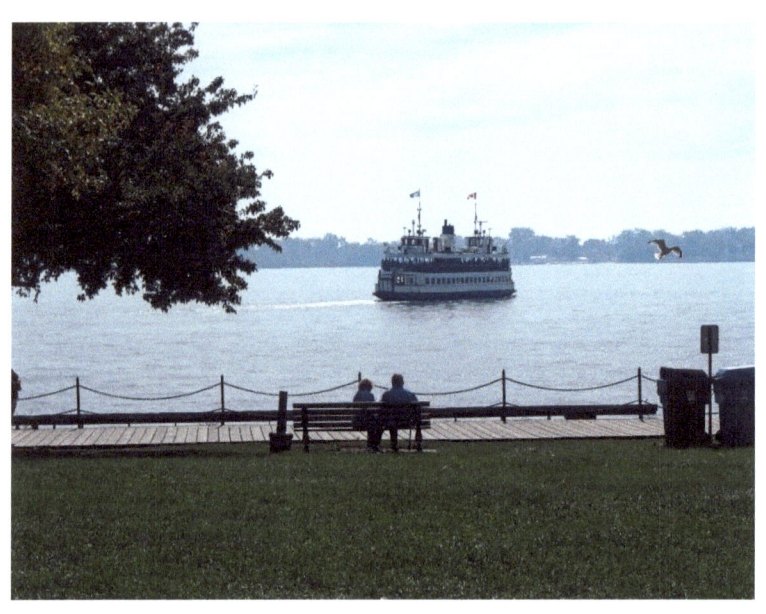

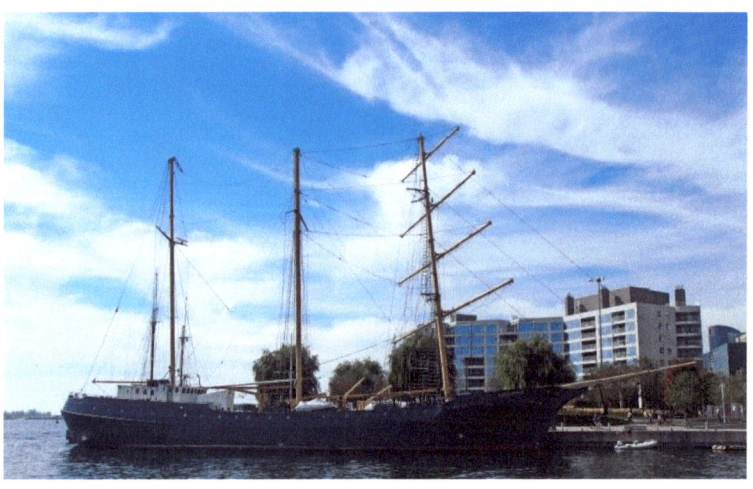

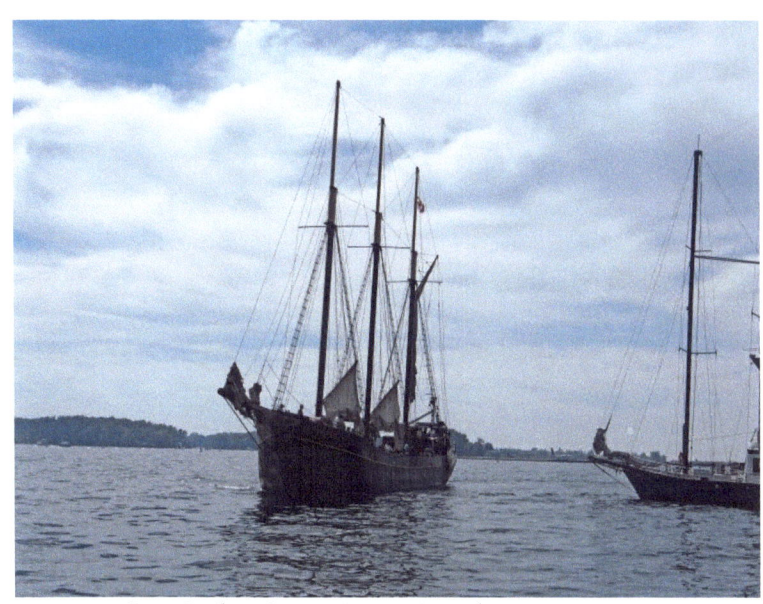

Our Lake Ontario cruise ship – Kajama

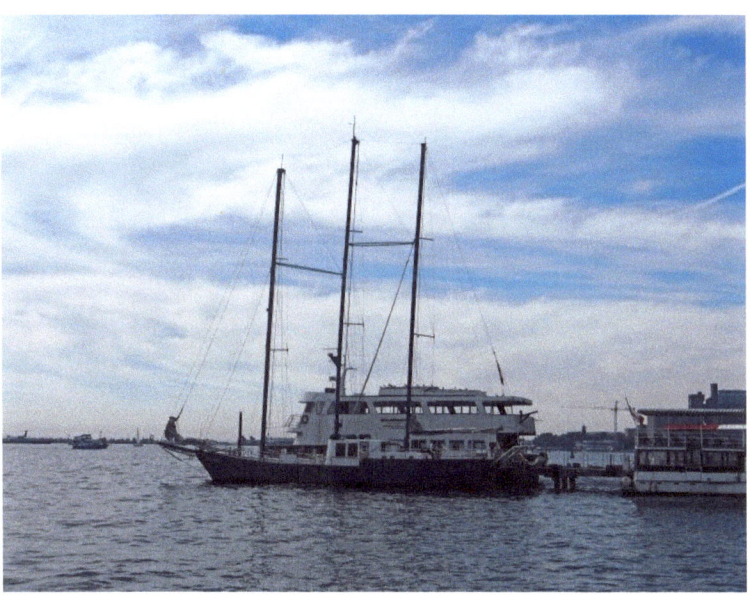

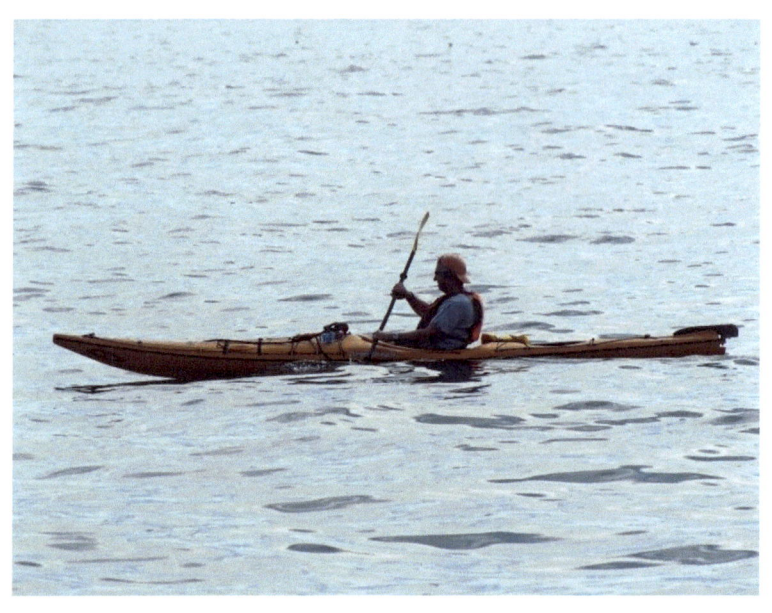

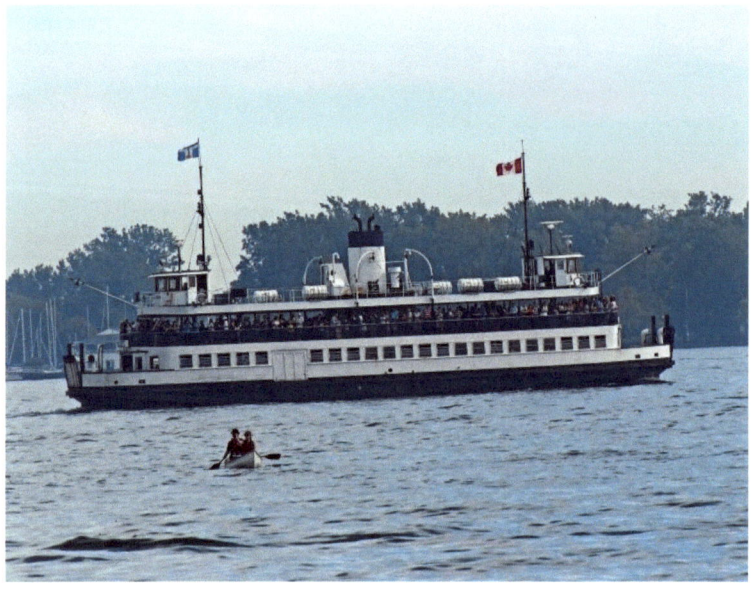

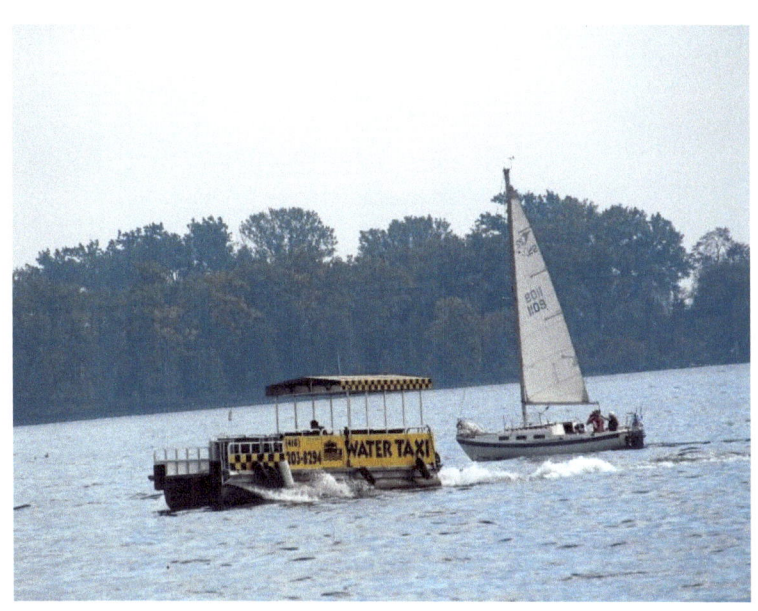

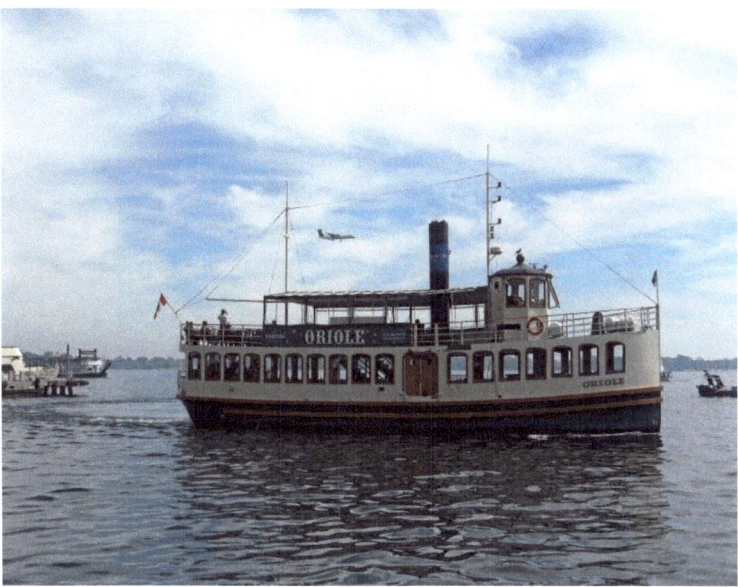

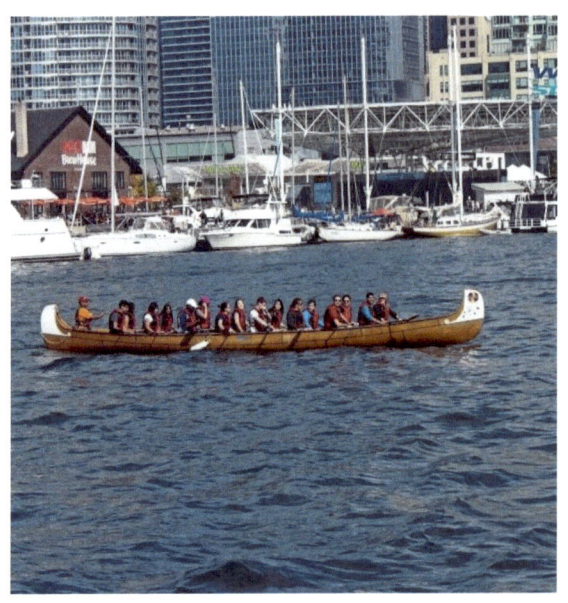

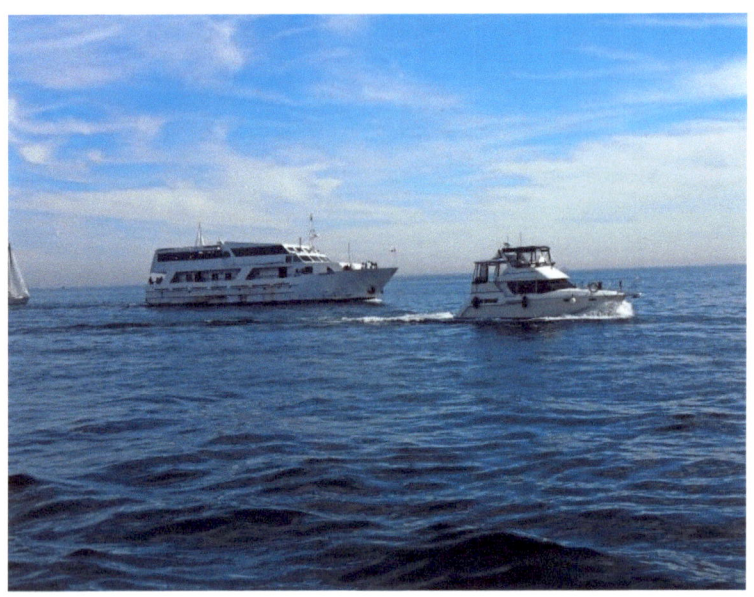

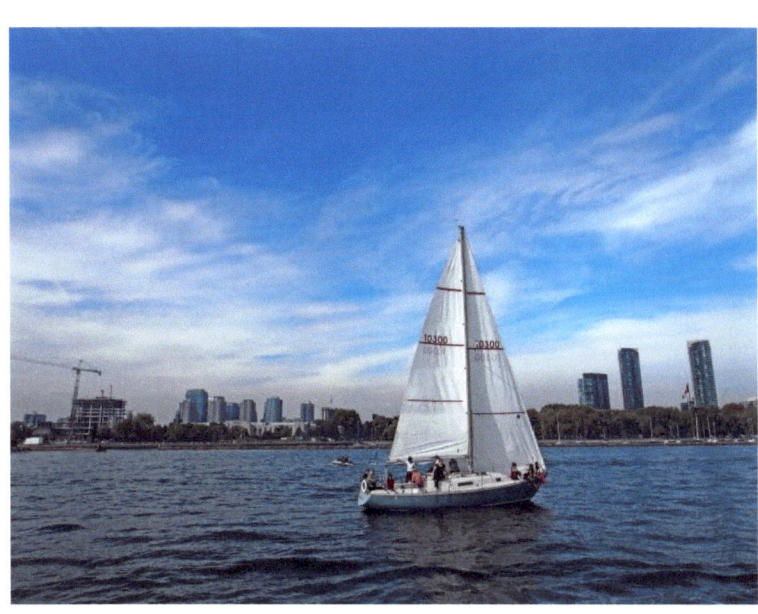

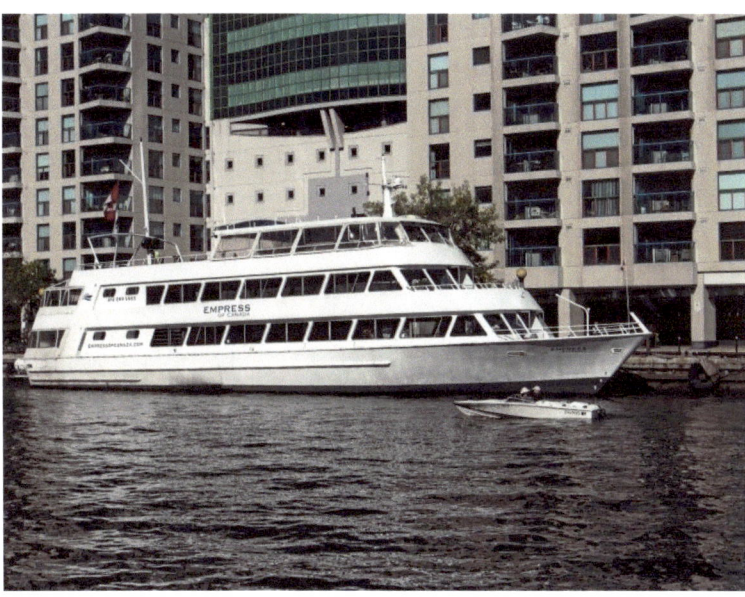

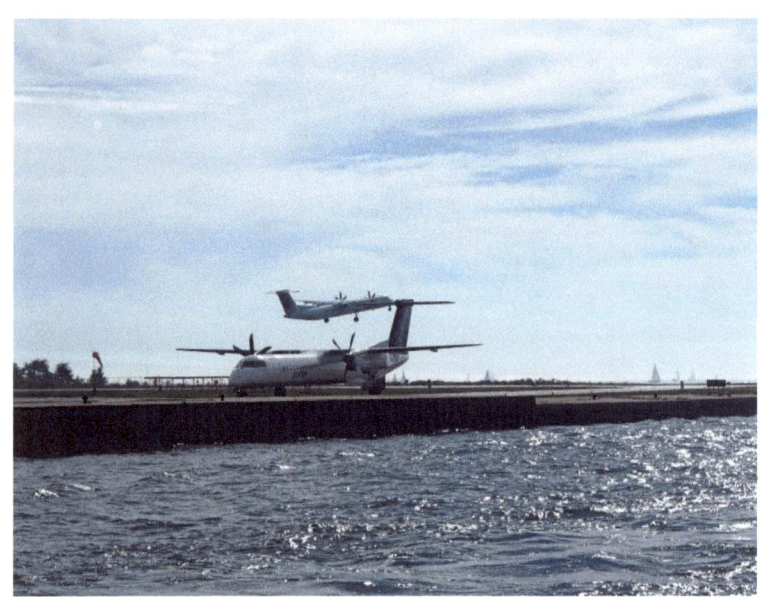

Billy Bishop Toronto City Airport

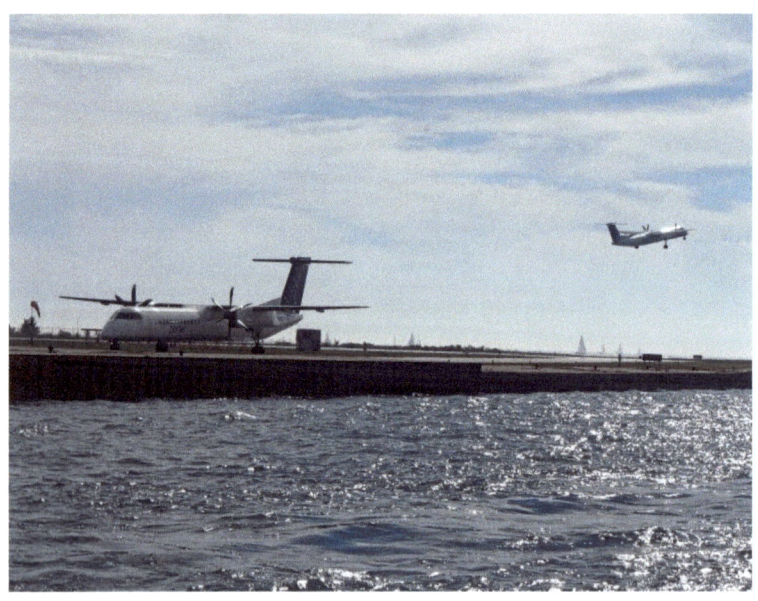

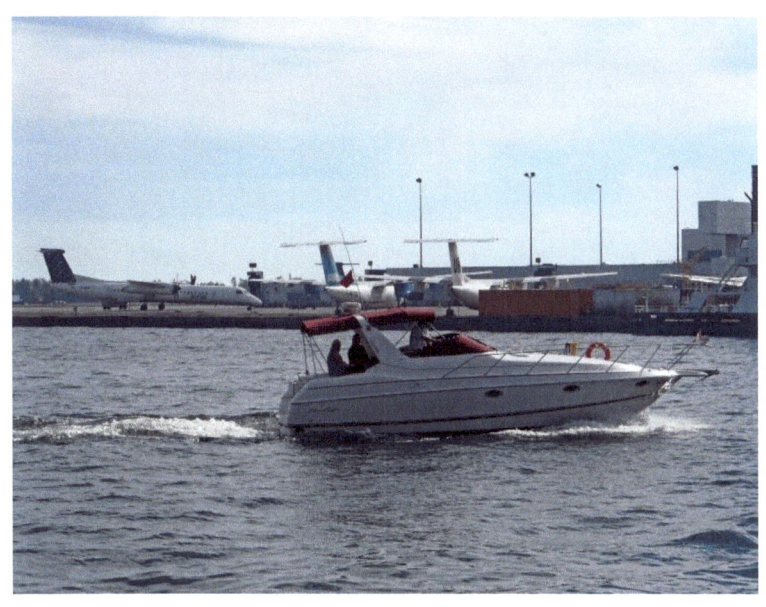

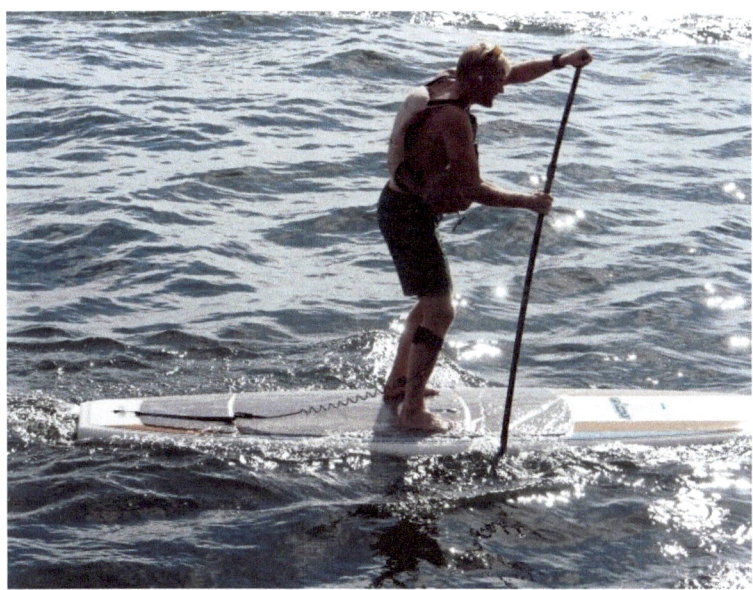

www.ingramcontent.com/pod-product-compliance
Lightning Source LLC
Chambersburg PA
CBHW040233220526
45473CB00001B/220